Robert Fellowes

A Picture of Christian Philosophy

Robert Fellowes

A Picture of Christian Philosophy

ISBN/EAN: 9783337025403

Printed in Europe, USA, Canada, Australia, Japan

Cover: Foto ©Lupo / pixelio.de

More available books at **www.hansebooks.com**

A PICTURE OF CHRISTIAN PHILOSOPHY.

BY
ROBERT FELLOWES, A.B. OXON.

THE SECOND EDITION,
WITH
CORRECTIONS AND CONSIDERABLE ADDITIONS.

Certainly it is heaven upon earth, to have a man's mind move in Charity, rest in Providence, and turn upon the poles of Truth.

LORD BACON.

London,
PRINTED FOR JOHN WHITE, BOOKSELLER, HORACE'S HEAD, FLEET-STREET.

1799.

PREFACE
TO THE FIRST EDITION.

A Principal design of the present publication is, by a delineation of the character of Jesus, to display the genuine unsophisticated spirit of his religion; and to shew what ought to be it's influence on the affections and the conduct of men in private life and in public stations. Some philosophers of our times have recommended a spirit of universal philanthropy, to the extinction of all local and individual partialities.* I have

---

* Among the most singular of these is Mr. Godwin, author of an elaborate work, called "Political Justice." Mr. G. certainly possesses great vigor of mind; but how often does he become a mere dreamer of dreams, and a compounder of absurdities! His system is totally impracticable; and even if it were practicable it would be pernicious:— it would abolish all the endearments of love and charity, and steel the human heart against it's best sympathies, with a more than stoical insensibility.

endeavoured to show, that though Christianity inspires universal benevolence, it encourages those individual sympathies which are it's foundation; and without which, universal philanthropy is but as a " sounding brass or a tinkling cymbal." The name of philanthropy may make a sweet sound, but it is but a sound without the observance of the lesser charities.

Many have represented the Christian temper as of the morose and sullen kind; and have thought it criminal for a Christian to engage in the bustle of the world, and to share in the gaieties of life. But the example of Jesus sanctions no such conclusions. He did not make fasting and prayer the key to heaven. He did not enjoin the sad but the cheerful countenance. Habits of solemn devotion he commanded and he practised; but his example proves that, that species of devotion is most agreeable to heaven, which abounds most in acts of beneficence to man.

The builders of theological systems seem usually to have paid too much attention to the writings of St. Paul, and too little to the doctrines and the practice of Christ; but I think that a modern believer has very little concern with the epistles of the Apostle. Those epistles were written on particular occasions and on temporary topics, to combat the fleeting heresies, the local and personal corruptions of the day. They can, therefore, but seldom be applied to the general doctrines of Christianity. Had Christians uniformly attended to this, we should probably never have heard of that distinction between faith and charity, with which enthusiasts have polluted pure Christianity.

A Christian ought exclusively to consider what were the doctrines, and what was the practice of Jesus; which may easily be collected from the accounts which the Evangelists have left us of his actions and his discourses; and according to these we ought, as much as possible, to regulate our doctrine, our affections and our practice. The doctrines of Jesus, as they have been delivered by the Evangelists, are plain and simple to all capacities; but the epistles, filled with allusions to evanescent topics, and to schisms which no longer disturb the church, are involved in a ten-fold obscurity, in which even sagacity and learning will be for ever bewildered. Why then, when we can walk in the light, should we prefer stumbling in darkness? Is it because we delight more in error than in truth? or because we imagine that there is no piety, where there is no mystery?

Another cause which has greatly contributed to obscure the true genius of the Christian system, is, that the majority of those who have set themselves down to the study of the subject, have rather endeavoured to make Christianity conform to their opinions, than make their opinions conform to Christianity. Slaves to some darling theory or some early prepossessions, they have rather sought for texts to confirm these, than to elucidate the truth by rational and dispassionate enquiry.

This is a principal reason why we have so many schemes of Christianity, and so many sects of Christians. Individuals, instead of endeavouring to discover the truth, as it is in Jesus, have endeavoured to pervert it, to their own narrow prejudices and partial views. But I trust that we have arrived at an age, when the enquirers into the doctrines of revelation, no longer blinded by the obstinacy of bigotry or the credulity of superstition, will cheerfully relinquish error to embrace truth; and will be less directed by vanity than by love to God and to mankind. Had the evidences and tenets of the Christian religion been constantly investigated with these affections, and with no other bias than a bias to benevolence, Skepticism could never have prevailed so much in the world; there would have been less bitterness and discordancy among believers; and infidelity would, at least, have wanted one subject of triumph, in the implacable animosities of Christians against Christians.

It is an absurd and a dangerous notion, that we can serve the cause of revelation by limiting the right of free discussion, or checking it by persecution. Persecution always increases the evil it is intended to remedy; and religious opinions, which respect the intercourse between man and his maker, ought for ever to be free from human interruption. They are too sacred for the cognizance of any earthly tribunal.

There seems to be a principle in human nature, ever jealous of the least usurpation on the right of private judgment, particularly in religious concerns; and which, though it often seem irregular and capricious in it's operations, was yet providently planted in us, by divine wisdom, as a strong auxiliary to truth, and a counteracting cause of tyranny and persecution. Had not mankind possessed this principle of counteraction, Christianity, when the miraculous effusions of the Holy Spirit had ceased, might have sunk lifeless and exhausted under successive persecutions. Truths, the most useful to mankind, which have commonly been attacked at their first appearance, by bigotry or by malice, might have perished as soon as they were born, and the moral and the intellectual world might have been covered with darkness. It was this principle which animated Luther and the early reformers, and shook the solid and artfully cemented fabric of Popery to it's base. It is this principle, which arming the conscience and the reason of man with an energy, proportionate to the fury that opposes their free exercise, has so often caused the diffusion of opinions, to keep pace with the rage that has struggled for their suppression.

As it is the collision of mind with mind, that discovers new truths and elucidates old, Christians ought by no means to discourage the discussion of the evidences of their religion. They ought rather to court such discussion, and engage in it themselves, without any of that spirit of bitterness, which often disgraces even the advocates of a good cause, and degrades the investigation of sacred truths into a petty personal contention.

Truth should be sought for truth's sake; not for the pleasure of exposing an adversary, or for the glory of victory, but for the sake of diminishing error and of diffusing knowledge. And surely the truths of Christianity, of all others, ought not to be discussed with rancour, but in the mild spirit of him from whom they came. The Christian ought to answer argument by argument, and not to seek the energies of logic in the vindictiveness of persecution. Let the believer and the unbeliever know, that Christianity can stand by argument; that it can derive no strength from rage and persecution; and that,

that only deserves the name of faith which is founded on sober and rational conviction.

It is full time that the evil spirit of persecution should be laid at rest for ever. After the experience of eighteen centuries, it is time that mankind should at last be convinced, that opinions, if true, can never be vanquished by oppression, and if false, many a melancholy page in history might have taught us, that human errors yield more certainly to mildness than to rage, to reason than to punishment.*

---

* When a political system is getting into disrepute, there seems to me to be but one way to retrieve it's character and to maintain it's authority; and that is, by making the people in general feel the happiness it produces, and their interest in supporting it.

When the benevolent Count Rumford undertook to reform the moral sentiments of the Bavarian beggars, he first rendered them easy and comfortable in their circumstances. A man is never so much averse to morality as when he is starving with hunger. That distress which is irretrievable breaks the spirit of independence, the source of honest and virtuous endeavour, and produces the lowest state of moral degradation. In this abject state, the individual, ceasing to perceive the blessings of civil order, grows impatient of it's restraints and anxious for it's dissolution. He becomes fit for all kinds of atrocities! If easy circumstances do not always produce morality, they are, at least, most favour-

Christian charity should incline us to forbearance towards each other; christian humility ought long ago to have instructed mankind, that those who claim the right of persecuting others for their opinions, are themselves as fallible as those they persecute. Let us have done with

---

able to it's production; for he who is in a state of wretchedness, approaching to despair, can hardly fail of being hostile to those laws of political justice, which constitute the individuality of property, and which are the strong base of social morality, and the sacred cement of civil government. No revolution could possibly take place in that country, where every individual was interested in the preservation of civil order; or, in other words, was attached by a reciprocal interest, to the practice of the duties of reciprocal justice. The governors of mankind cannot give too much attention to this principle, if they wish to identify their own power with the interests and the affections of the people, and to unite all the gradations of civil society, by the connecting bond of a sympathetic benevolence.

A communion of happiness is not only not incompatible with a disparity of property, but is inattainable without it. The greatest happiness which mankind can enjoy on earth, arises from a benevolent intercourse with each other. Were all men equal in circumstances, there would be no room for a reciprocity of kindnesses. A disparity of conditions occasions a disparity of wants, and gives rise to most of the affections which gladden life. The complicated and diversified circumstances of mankind warm into life and stimulate into action those benevolent sympathies which are the ornaments of our species, and the prolific causes of a reciprocity of happiness. Without them we should be absorbed in a brutal selfishness, and acquainted with none but the lowest animal enjoyments.

that vehement, dogmatifing, intolerant and fanguinary fpirit, which in former ages burned it's victims in the flames; and which, in the prefent, has opened far and wide the fluices of human gore, and filled the earth with fpectacles of mifery!!!

The times themfelves, by their awful and tremendous afpect, portending the wrath of heaven on our prefumption, our animofity and our crimes, ought to induce us to return to a fyftem of reciprocal benevolence and moderation. To fuffer a mere difference of opinion to make us as hoftile to each other, as if we were beings of a different fpecies, appears a ftrange mockery of the religion we profefs; whofe features are mildnefs, and whofe precepts are love.

Were the defolating animofity, which at this moment feparates from each other ftates and individuals, to be perpetual, even a righteous man might be almoft tempted to loath exiftence! But let us hope, that thefe days, dark and difmal as they now appear, will be fhortened by the All-wife and All-good Difpenfer of individual and of national felicity. Though at this moment the world be teeming with revolutions, though thrones be tottering to their fall, though changes the moft important have happened fo rapidly, that they almoft appear as the vifions of a dream, let us with calm refignation, truft that the Divine Providence is bufily employed in this folemn drama; arranging all it's parts on the wifeft plans, and difpofing them, notwithftanding the gloomy fadnefs of intermediate diforders, for a conclufion, favourable to virtue, to piety and to happinefs.

HARBURY,
April 3, 1798.

PREFACE
TO THE SECOND EDITION.

THE favourable reception of the first edition of this work, has encouraged the author to publish the present, enlarged, and he hopes, improved edition. The manner, in which he has treated the most important of all subjects, has, he trusts, however displeasing it may have been to some few individuals, been generally approved.

The lovers of bitterness, the fomenters of animosity, and the champions of intolerance will take no pleasure in the following pages; but the author hopes, that the friends of revealed truth and of human happiness will not have occasion to regret either the expence of the publication, or the time it may employ. The author is not the timid or obsequious votary of any party.

He has not been scrupulously delicate about adjusting his opinions to the standard of fashion; careless of personal favour or emolument, he has sedulously sought for truth in the sanctuary of the scriptures. Instead of tuning the harmony of his notions to the breath of every fleeting interest; he has endeavoured, with unfeigned sincerity, to direct the steps of his fellow creatures, by the torch of Christian love, to life eternal. If by the grace of Divine Providence, without which the author has an undoubting conviction that *all his exertions must be fruitless,* he is made the instrument of spreading the unsullied light of the true gospel, or of exciting the flame of genuine benevolence in only one individual, he will feel a happiness which wealth could not give, and which poverty cannot take away.

ROBERT FELLOWES,

Curate of Harbury, near Southam, Warwickshire.

February 15, 1799.

CONTENTS.

TEXT.

PAGES

1. THE character of Jesus, as it has been represented by the four Evangelists, an argument for the truth of Christianity.

1—4. The character of Christ not fictitious; arises out of the discourses, incidents, &c. connected with it; drawn by four different hands; who, amid particular variations, agree exactly in the general and individual likeness. The variations prove the absence of any concert between the historians. Such concert necessary, if they had not described the same original.

5, 6. The opinion, that the variations were the effect of collusion, supposes talents for imposture, incompatible with the simplicity of the Evangelists.

6—11. On the supposition, that the discourses, &c. of Jesus are a mixture of truth and fable; the difficulty of distinguishing the one from the other, from the identity of character that pervades both.

12. The genuineness of the discourses involves the truth of the miracles.

PAGES		
13		Considerations on the marks of energy and authority that characterised the manner of Jesus; and of which the features are accurately preserved in the narrative of the Evangelists.
13	14	Jesus taught as one having authority. Contrast between the speaker and his circumstances.
14	15	Character of imposture. Had Jesus been an impostor, he must have blended consummate arrogance with consummate art. The different impressions of false and genuine authority. The triumph of the latter over physical power.
	15	Cæsar conscious of the authority of Cicero; anxious to obtain advantage of it.
	16	In Louis the XVIth, the authority of his manner survived the wreck of his power.
16—18		The authority of Jesus impressive, without being assisted by any lustre of talents or of station. His energetic manner marked with singular accuracy and discrimination, by the four Evangelists.
19	20	The grandeur of his manner did not accord with the poorness of his circumstances. In his actual circumstances, Jesus, without divine energies, would have provoked derision.
20	21	The multitude judge by outward appearances. The contemptuousness of Christ's outward appearance vanished in the essential dignity of his manner; and which caused his sayings to be heard with attention.
21—23		Instances, in which the energy of his manner, palsied the power of his enemies; adapted to the character, the character to them, not likely to have been fabricated; corroborate the truth of the narrative.
23	24	No discrepancies in the manner of Jesus.

	25	Remarks on the Christian miracles.
25	26	The Christian miracles analogous to the other operations of the Deity; if fictitious, would have proved their own refutation.

PAGES	
27 28	Supposing them the fabrications of the historians; they have related so many lies with as much apparent veracity as they could facts, of which they were eye-witnesses. Their consciousness of truth evinced by their making no provisions against objections.
28	Truth characterised by intrepidity, falshood by the subterfuges of fear.
28 29	The character of the miracles corresponds with the purpose of the revelation.
30 31	Distinctions between forged and real history. Difficulties to success in the former. The consistency and veracity of the Evangelists.

———◦———

32	*Remarks on the miracle of the blind man restored to sight by Jesus, according to the account given by St. John ix.*
32 33	The blind man seen by Jesus; the question of the Apostles; remarks on the introduction to the miracle.
33 34	Answer of Jesus; characterised by confidence and energy. His custom of giving, incidentally, the most weighty counsels.
35	Jesus effects the cure by clay mixed with spittle; not the act of an impostor.
36—39	Instead of lavishing any panegyric on the physician, the Evangelist details a very natural and animated enquiry into the reality of the cure.
39 40	The man who had been blind, declares that Jesus had restored his sight. He is brought before the Pharisees, relates his cure; they call his parents.
40 41	Remarks on the proceedings of the Pharisees; they question the parents; referred back to the son. The circumstantiality of the narrative.
41 42	The Pharisees artfully endeavour to divert the attention from the author of the miracle. The answer of him, who had received his sight, to the peremptory assertion of the Pharisees; remarks on it.

PAGES

42 43   The Pharisees incensed; their passionate interrogatories. Their impatience represented to the life. Their vehemence stimulates the poor man to greater boldness of speech. He is reviled by the Pharisees. Boldly defends Jesus. Their rage inflamed; they cast him out.

43—45   The dialogue that follows the miracle corroborates it's reality. Great dexterity exhibited in the representation of this miracle, supposing it a fiction. The author's wish that his remarks on it may serve the cause of revelation.

---

46   *The character of Jesus illustrated.*

46   Early impressions lay the foundation of character.

47—50   The circumstances in which Jesus was placed, in early life, not favourable to the production of such a character.

50—54   Jesus, not initiated in the learning of the Jews; not infected with the national prejudices that prevailed in his time; he had either erased the impressions of his youth, or was, by the divine favour, exempted from their influence.

54—56   A general sketch of his character. Conspicuous for the passive virtues; their excellence; do not exclude more energetic qualities.

56 57   Jesus commends those virtues, which do not dazzle by their splendour; the pattern of his own lessons; acquainted with the efficient causes of human happiness; his instructions calculated to promote it.

57 58   Revenge predominant in the savage state; religion only, can abate it's ferocity; physical causes which promote it's expansion; perverse associations inflame it to fury.

58 59   Human happiness essentially connected with benevolent sympathy.

59 60   Jesus, the only recorded victor of the revengeful passions; meekness recommended by his example.

60—64   Our present associations pass with us into other states of being; the importance of this consideration.

64—66   The humility of Jesus; an impressive instance of it.

PAGES	
67 68	Kind attention to little children, characteristic of benevolence; so considered by Jesus.
69	The Evangelists make no parade of eloquence.
69 70	Jesus heals Peter's wife's mother; heals the centurion's servant; his promptitude in doing good.
70—72	A ruler of the synagogue beseeches Jesus to heal his daughter. News of her death. Jesus comforts the distracted father; arrives at the ruler's house; the delicacy of his benevolence.
72—74	A dead corpse. The parents and spectators weep. Jesus represents the deceased in a trance. The irritability of the mind in a state of great affliction. Jesus derided. The dead raised.
74—76	The tenderness of Jesus exemplified, near the city of Nain; the funeral procession of a widow's only son. The misery of the mother. Jesus comforts her; his style of condolence; he raises the deceased.
76—78	The beneficence of Jesus full of life and energy; heightened by the kindness of his manner; never lost sight of individual misery. The rule of the *general good*, not suited to the practical purposes of life.
78—80	The "general good" not an object of sympathy. Sympathy prompts to the relief of individuals. The relations of friendship, &c. not to be sacrificed to the interest of the community.
80 81	Mr. Godwin's rule of life more fallible and mischievous than that of sympathy. The rule of life proposed by our Saviour.
81 82	Virtue consists in serving the detail of society. The quantity of public happiness more increased by individuals, aiming at partial than at general good.
82—88	Universal benevolence, inseparable from individual attachments; association produces them. The gradual expansion of our affections. Partial without universal, universal without partial benevolence.
89 91	Particular affections, give birth to general. In Jesus, universal did not absorb partial love.
91	The domestic affections a cordial to the heart.
91—93	Friendship derives it's energy from sympathy. Kindred love strengthened by intercourse.

PAGES

93—95　True friendship partakes of the sacredness of kindred love. Jesus sanctions the flame of private friendship. His conduct on the death of Lazarus. He receives intelligence of Lazarus's sickness; delays visiting him. Lazarus dies. Why, Jesus would not see him in his last sickness.

95—98　Martha goes to meet Jesus. Mary sits still. The unity and consistency of *their* characters. Jesus tells Martha, that her brother shall live again; she fetches her sister. Jesus deeply affected. The Jews remark his affection for Lazarus. He proceeds to the tomb, raises the dead. Eulogy on his friendship.

98　99　Jesus not negligent of kindred love. Providence wills family love. Sympathy improves it;—a source of exquisite happiness.

99—104　Conjugal love productive of happiness; Christian restraints on marriage; it's religious obligations; only adultery can justify it's dissolution. Mischievous consequences of separating marriage from the Christian sanctions. Habitual intercourse smooths off the incongruities of temper, &c.—Conjugal affection, want of in brutes; it's interesting appearance in mankind. The transports of fancy short-lived. Mutual esteem lasts thro' life. Pure affection renewed after death.

104—109　The patriotic affections, their use; capable of universal diffusion. A good Christian will love his country; but will not sacrifice justice and benevolence to the principle of patriotism.

109　110　Nations interested in the prosperity of their neighbours. The want of benevolence blinds mankind to their true interests.

110　A good Christian will not be an advocate for offensive war; will cheerfully die for the liberties of his country.

111—113　Traits of patriotic affection in Jesus.

113　A good Christian will maintain the cause of public virtue and of genuine piety.

114—119　The pretended Evangelical preachers have injured Christianity. Their instructions different from those of Jesus.

119—128　Mr. Wilberforce's opinion of the corruption of human nature.—The doctrine of imputed sin, contrary to our natural

(xxiii)

PAGES

sense of justice. We do not inherit sin by descent from Adam; not objects of punishment, till we have sinned in our own persons. The curse passed upon Adam. The law to which he was subject in Paradise. The consequences of transgressing it. Sin, the violation of a known law. Guilt, reflected from a sense of duty. The doctrine of imputed sin, subversive of moral rectitude; gives unworthy notions of God; not insisted on by Jesus or his Apostles.

129—134 St. Paul, character of.

134 135 Every necessary part of Christian knowledge contained in the four Gospels and Acts. The reason why Christianity is less plain now than it was at first.

135—139 The discourses of Jesus inculcate practical goodness. His miracles, lessons of benevolence. Opportunities of beneficence not to be neglected. The parables of Jesus, their practical tendency.

139—146 Diverse opinions on the redemption of man. Immortality the free gift of God; conditions appended to it; all comprehended in Charity. The precise nature of the atonement inexplicable. "To keep the commandments," of more importance than to dive into the perplexities of mystery.

146—154 Jesus prays in retirement. Solitude congenial to devotion. It's spirit languishes without exercise, frequent abstraction from sensual objects, prevents corruption; gives strength to advance in holiness. In prayer, the thoughts should not wander from the divine presence. The devotion of Jesus, marked by earnestness and solemnity. His prayer in the garden of Gethsemane. Devotion the source of consolation. Prayer ought not to supplant religious *practice*. Characteristic features of true devotion.

154 The government of the thoughts, a religious duty. Licentious ideas, their mischievous tendency.

155—158 Christianity, friendly to innocent cheerfulness. It's spirit contrasted with that of Calvinism.

158—164 Theatrical amusements, their tendency, &c. considered.

164 The affections, a fallacious test of religion.

PAGES

165—170 Divine love and social the same. The union of morality and religion. Benevolence absorbs selfishness. The selfish counteracts the social principle. The influence of the latter; fostered by the relations of nature, &c. Christianity favours the social flame; sanctions benevolence. Benevolent sympathy, the sum of religion.

170—171 Devout sensation encouraged; the associate of true holiness, to be kept distinct from enthusiastic fervor.

172—178 Gratitude ought to be cherished; description of a grateful man. Gratitude to God described. Jesus calls mutual love a new commandment. The essential principle of his doctrine. Has been grossly neglected in the Christian world. Brotherly love of more consequence than modes of faith. The consecrating and consecrated element of Christian piety.

---

179 *Jesus on the cross, a martyr to truth.*

179 The death of Jesus and of Socrates.

180—182 Jesus prays for his enemies. A picture of the tortured Indian. Revenge his ruling passion. His insensibility contrasted with the tenderness of Jesus.

182—183 Sympathy, implies a reciprocity of sensation. We sympathise with the sufferings of Jesus.

183—187 Jesus suffered for the truth. Truth, never mischievous; counteracted by the malignity of error; not to impute to the tho first the evils that belong to the last.

187—190 Truth and falshood do not vary with circumstances. The contrary supposition. Every interest secondary to that of truth. Truth ought not to crouch to human policy. To be defended at every hazard.

---

191 *A future life---an immaterial principle---the truth of the resurrection of Jesus---practical inferences, &c.*

191—197 An immaterial principle not discoverable by the light of nature. The mind seems the product of material organs.

PAGES

The senses our only medium of knowledge. Ideas, called abstract, have a sensual original. Abstract terms, abbreviations. No abstract ideas. The mind appears to perish with the body.

197—205 The principle of volition; whence it results; sympathises with the changes of the body; does not survive it.

205—208 A principle of consciousness. Memory and consciousness compared. Consciousness not affected by the waste and changes of the body; probably distinct from the animal organization; St Paul's spiritual body.

208—211 In the natural world no analogies of a continuation of consciousness. Without such a continuation, no revival of the individual.

211—213 The general expectation of a future life, no proof of it; how excited; a ray of consolation emitted from it. The more dark the intimations of a future state from the light of nature, the more probable a particular communication from the Deity, on the subject.

213—216 The fact of the resurrection of Jesus supported by " priori," as well as " posteriori " evidence. The truth of any miracle depends on the arguments for the fact; not on previous considerations on the general course of nature. General laws compatible with moral government.

216—218 The Christian miracles consonant to the laws of the moral world. Mr. Hume's objection. The converse of his celebrated proposition true.

218—221 The fact of the resurrection consonant to the most enlarged notions of the divine wisdom and goodness. That the Almighty would communicate intelligence of a future life, probable from the faint and imperfect distinctions between vice and virtue in this world. The knowledge of a future state, necessary for moral purposes.

222—224 Provision made by nature in favour of truth. Men never impostors and liars without a motive. The motives of the Apostles?

224—227 The love of life energises the principle of self-interest. The different modifications and directions of self-interest.

PAGES	
	The motives of the Apostles must be referred to a future interest, grounded on the conviction, that Jesus was risen from the dead.
228—231	Assent to testimony, proportioned to the credibility of the witnesses. The Apostles not inclined to credulity. The pains which Jesus took to manifest the reality of his resurrection.
231—235	The Apostles boldly assert the truth of the *resurrection*, before the Jewish rulers. St. Paul's conversion a proof of it.
235—240	The recorded testimony of the Apostles is that which they delivered to the world; has not been impaired by time.
240—242	Objection to the fact of the resurrection, from the constant uniformity of the laws of nature. Our knowledge of *their* past uniformity, rests on the credit of testimony.
242 243	Christianity demands an assent to testimony, on rational principles. The benefit of calm investigation. Objection, that present experience confirms the past uniformity of the laws of nature, and shakes the credibility of the resurrection.
243—246	Testimony, alone, proves the identity between the present and past state of the physical and moral world. The great mass of that knowledge true. The Skeptic exhorted to examine the testimony in favour of the resurrection.
246—248	The Apostles persevered, in the midst of tortures, in affirming the truth of the resurrection. If that resurrection was not true; unqualified wretchedness the object of their vigorous pursuit. Such conduct as improbable as that a dead man should rise to life.
248 249	The conduct of the Apostles confirms the truth of the miracles; and the integrity of their testimony.
249 250	It is more probable that the testimony in favour of the resurrection should be true, than the fact false. Moral as well as natural laws. The resurrection of Jesus consonant to the first; the probable analogy of both.
250—255	The truth of the resurrection; it's practical importance: Incites to disinterested benevolence, &c. Christian hope.

PAGES	
256	*Thoughts on the free discussion of the evidences of revelation.*
256—262	Conviction proportioned to the degree of knowledge. Faith according to conviction. The evidences of revelation so arranged, that enquiry must precede conviction; the uses of such enquiry. We are to pray for unbelievers. Their arguments to be refuted; impotency of their abuse and ribaldry. Revelation not intended to rule by constraint, but choice. Discussion favourable to it's interests.
263 264	*Postscript.*

CONTENTS.

NOTES.

PAGES	
4 5	Minute differences, in the relation of the same fact, by different individuals, do not destroy it's credibility. Historians, sometimes, relate events in an order different from their natural.
6	Matthew, Mark, and Luke had not seen each other's gospels. John wrote more particularly to explain the divine nature of Christ.
7—9	Language inadequate to represent all the tints and changes of sensation. The imperfections of picturesque description. The stock of epithets scanty and defective.
10 11	Gothic architecture; in what it excells the Grecian. Gothic churches, representations of woods, caves, &c.
15	Political distinction between power and authority.
17	References to passages in the Evangelists, in which the authoritative manner of Jesus appears in a strong light.
25—26	Useful inferences, from our Saviour's two miracles of destruction.
36	Not a particle of adulation in the Gospel-history.
36—38	Men tinge the language in which they write with the language in which they think. The Greek of the Evangelists marked with Hebraisms;—an argument against the plenary inspiration of Scripture. The variations in the Evangelic memoirs, arguments for their credibility, as human compositions, contrary to the supposition of a plenary inspiration. The construction of Scripture to be adapted to the Eastern idiom.
45	Conclusion of the miracle of the blind man.

PAGES

46—50 Genius arises from early sympathy. Antipathies caused by perverse associations. Reason often a feeble antagonist to sensation. The influence of incidental impressions survives the remembrance of the impression. Knowledge of the power of early association; it's importance. Formation of a benevolent character.—Every species of gaming injurious to the benevolent principle.

58 53 The obstinacy of prejudice. **Causes which operate** against the discovery of truth. The difficulty of forming just **notions** on religious subjects. Differences of opinion in **religion,** ought not to hinder mutual charity and forbearance.

61—64 The revival of consciousness, a renewal of past associations. Our next state will be a state of improvement. The benevolent and malevolent will pass into different regions.—The *eternity of punishments* cannot be reconciled to our knowledge of the divine attributes. The language of Scripture, on that subject, probably figurative. The use of punishment;—that of the wicked will be of long continuance.

83 Howard, Count Rumford, Darwin, and Beddoes celebrated.
84—86 Burke, character of.
86—88 Rousseau, on his character and writings.
89—91 Peter, the Apostle, his character.
91 John, his benevolence.
106—107 The power of association over the affections. The origin of our attachment to particular forms, &c.
111 Jesus not an advocate for political servitude. The right construction of his reply to the question of the Jews: "Is it lawful," &c.
114—119 Extract from a MS. of Chatterton, on the Trinity. The life and writings of Chatterton.
127 128 The doctrine of imputed sin has obstructed the progress of Christianity.
135 136 The artifice and folly of the pretended Evangelical preachers.
139 140 Quotations from St. John and St. Matt.
143 Jesus, the source of eternal life.
144 145 Vital benevolence, the religion most pleasing to God.
147 Quotations from Mark and Matt.

PAGES

148   The moral as well as the physical taste naturally good; liable to be vitiated.

155   Count Rumford's opinion of cleanliness of body. Filthy thoughts, &c. corrupt the moral principle.

162   Modesty commended, from Med. Ext.

184 185   The majority of minds passive. Human knowledge, in general, a mass of prejudices. The produce of truth, proportionate to the extent and vigor of enquiry. The augmentation of knowledge tends to it's simplification.

192 193   The sense of touch, on it's degrees of excitability in animals and men. Perception, a modification of sensation. The other senses, a modification of the same power, which constitutes the sense of touch.

196 197   Importance of fixing *definite* significations to words. Taste and intelligence shewn in using them with fitness, and combining them with beauty. Education rightly begun by teaching the signification of words; pains should be taken to excite the particular sensations they express.

197—202   Energy of volition calls forth vigor of intellect.—Agreeable sensation the chief pursuit of man.—Early sympathy associates the idea of *agreeable sensation* with *particular* pursuits. This stimulates volition; and leads to excellence. Genius may be created. Various reflections on the subject. Why Sir J. Reynolds excelled in painting. Eagerness never evinced in any pursuit not associated with agreeable sensation. What degree of encouragement favourable to genius? Cases in which neither favour nor neglect can wither the energies of the active principle.

202   Feebleness of volition in brutes.

203   Strength of memory depends on strength of volition.

205 206   The consciousness of *personality* never absent from us.

206   Significations of identity.

206 207   Renovation and decay of animal power.

207   The nature of the power of consciousness.

215   Prescience and Providence distinguished.

222   The love of truth in Children; how they come to associate

PAGES

falshood with the pleasures of self-interest. Thier early disclo-
sure of a love of truth.

223   The doctrine of counteracting motives, it's importance.
238   Various readings in Mills' New Testament.
251 252 Christianity makes self-interest centre in benevolence.
260 261 The assaults of Infidelity, not injurious to the Christian
cause. French Infidelity had it's origin in the corruptions of
Popery. The probable revival of pure Christianity in France.

ERRATA.

☞ THE Reader is requested to correct and pardon the following errata: the Author regrets that they are so numerous; but they were occasioned by circumstances, which he could not controul.

PAGE	LINE	
10	3	Note, for *wavering* read *waving*.
11	7	note, for *foilage* read *foliage*.
16	5	for *twhich the* read *which*.
19	5	for *devised* read *derived*.
19	7	for *saying* read *sayings*.
23	2	for *Evangelists* read *Evangelists*.
26	14	for *as* read *so*.
49	23	note, for *general* read *genial*.
61	10	note, for *will probably be* read *will be*.
62	18	note, for *disgust* read *distrust*.
81	17	for *map* read *mass*.
84	9	note, for *million* read *millions*.
86	29	note, for *not so profound* read *not profound*.
87	9	note, for *apathies* read *apathy*.
90	20	note, for *of the Apostles* read *of the other Apostles*.
90	21	note, for *emotions* read *emotion*.
92	3	for *sensations* read *sensation*.
93	6	for *to cast* read *to be cast*.
95	3	for *fullest* read *fittest*.
98	2	for *roofs* read *roots*.
99	22	for *x, xi.* read *xix*.
100	1	for *no* read *not*.
100	16	for *principle* read *principles*.
103	14	for *to the calmer* read *to calmer*.
103	20	for *leads* read *lass*.
105	5	for *and the* read *and of the*.
107	11	note, for *arises* read *raises*.
108	5	for *no limits* read *no other limits*.
104	14	for *in the waste* read *in this waste*.
109	4	for *misfortunes* read *misfortune*.
115	7	note, for *predilution* read *predilection*.
115	19	note, for *flept* read *slept*.
115	26	note, for *attribute* read *attribute*.
118	23	note, for *negneet* read *neglect*.
148	5	for *congenial to* read *congenial*.
193	1	note, for *supposistion* read *supposition*.
220	22	for *interest* read *interests*.
229	5	for *faculty* read *facility*.
233	4	for *that* read *had*.
236	7	for *changes or depredation* read *change or depredation*.

⁂ IN the perusal of the work, it is not improbable that the Reader will discover a few other errata; and for which, as well as those noticed above, the Author solicits his kind indulgence.

A PICTURE OF
CHRISTIAN PHILOSOPHY.

The character of Jesus, as it has been represented by the four Evangelists, an argument for the truth of Christianity.

THE character of Jesus, as it has been drawn by the Evangelists, affords a strong presumptive proof of the truth of Christianity. The features of it are so striking, and yet so consistent with each other, that it seems absurd, at first sight, to suppose it a fiction;— and a fiction of a few peasants and fishermen. Even the friends to infidelity must allow it to be the most singular character that is to be found in the annals of the world: and it's singularity does not arise so much from it's particular dissimilitude to others, as from it's superiority, in all particulars, to every character of which history has made any mention in any age. The writers of romance never even feigned a character so perfect and excellent. It was beyond the virtue of mortality to equal, and the wit of mortals to imagine.

The difficulty of giving harmony and confiftency to a feigned character, and to one placed in extraordinary circumftances, and reprefented as poffeffing extraordinary powers, will be acknowledged by all who ever made the effay in works of imagination.

The character of Jefus, is not drawn by the Evangelifts in the broad lines of vulgar panegyric; but in the artlefs and fimple touches of a delicate pencil. His praifes are not founded in our ears. His virtues are not particularifed; they are not even named; but they are more ftrongly imprinted in our minds, than if they had been lauded a thoufand times in all the fplendour of eloquence, by the difcourfes, the incidents and the actions of his life. And all thefe difcourfes, incidents and actions, fuppofing them a fiction, muft have been moft artfully and ably managed indeed! They are all made fo aptly to combine, as to reprefent the moft perfect unity and identity of character.

If, therefore, the Evangelists did not paint from life; if they have related discourses which were never delivered, incidents which never happened, features of character and shades of manners which they never beheld, they must have been, though confessedly without taste or literature, men of the most exquisite taste and discernment which were ever known. Had they no original before them, they have described an imagined resemblance most artfully, and yet most inartificially.

But can any candid examiner believe, that the Evangelists have painted a non-existence? will he not rather allow that they have delineated the discourses, actions and manners of Jesus, such as they were, and such as they witnessed them to be, in the language of candour, of truth and simplicity?

We are, besides, to consider — that the character of Jesus is not drawn by one person only; but by four different hands; all of whom, palpably, describe the same original. In particular circumstances, and, as it were, shades of their narration, they differ; but, amid a diversity of circumstances, they do not exhibit the least cast of a diversity of character.

This confideration is of great importance; becaufe, had they been defcribing a fictitious character only, it is more than probable, that their differences would have deftroyed the appearance of it's individuality and identity. But, at prefent, thefe differences take no more from the individual likenefs, than if feveral painters fhould reprefent the fame identic features, and only differ in a few minute folds or ornaments of the drapery.

The Evangelifts preferve a perfect confiftency and uniformity of character, amid a multitude of petty variations; and which variations only prove, that they did not write in concert; but that, like honeft men, they delivered the truth, and nothing but the truth, to the beft of their knowlege and conviction. But had they painted a non-exiftence, they muft have written in concert: for feveral perfons can never be fuppofed to have imagined a fimilar fiction, without the moft glaring difcordancies.* And, fuppofing that the Evangelifts did

---

* In the relation of the fame fact, by different individuals, it will always happen that fome particulars will be mentioned by one, which are omitted by another; and "vice verfa." But this is not fufficient to fhake the credibility of any narrative whatever. Were any one, at this moment,

write in concert, how are we to account for the particular diffimilitudes which are vifible in their narration?

It may be faid, that by an excefs of refinement in fraud, fuch diffimilitudes were the effect of collufion; but this collufion, of which there is not the leaft ap-

---

to fall down before my door and break his leg, and were twelve perfons prefent, it is more than probable that all the twelve would relate the fame fact in a fomewhat different way. They would differ in fome minute and incidental circumftances; but they would all agree, without the leaft variation, that the man broke his leg.

No one can have been much prefent in courts of juftice without obferving the incidental variations that are conftantly occurring in the teftimony of even honeft and credible witneffes. In the narrative of the refurrection, by the four Evangelifts, their feveral variations may be confidered either under the head of omiffions or additions; or as indiftinct difcriminations of the precife order of time, in which the incidental circumftances or ramifications of the fame event took place. It is by no means uncommon for hiftorians, either for the fake of a more lucid arrangement of their fubject, or of placing fome great event in a ftronger light; to invert the natural order of fome minute, immaterial and affociated occurrences, and to place them in an order different from their literal, arithmetical and chronological feries. It is by no means improbable, that the Evangelifts, in recording the refurrection, neglected fome of the leaft fractions of chronology. Hence there may arife fome apparent confufion in their feveral relations.

A 3

pearance, must be proved, before it can be believed;* and, could it be proved, it would render the Evangelists, in whom we cannot trace the least talents for imposture, the ablest impostors that ever conquered the credulity of mankind.

Which ever way the advocates for infidelity attempt to get rid of that argument for the truth of Christianity, which is supplied by a candid examination of the character of Jesus, they will, I am persuaded, find themselves involved in contradictions and absurdities; from which there is no escape, but by allowing the integrity of the relators and the truth of the relation.

Admitting the truth of the relation, the truth of the miraculous powers ascribed to Jesus, and the truth of

---

* There is reason to believe that neither Matthew, Mark, nor Luke had seen each other's gospels, at the time of writing their own. John seems to have written with a view to supply the omissions of the former Evangelists; and particularly to give us a farther insight into the nature of Christ's mission, and of his union with and dependance on the Father, than they had done. Hence, in considering the question of Christ's divinity, we should pay particular attention to St. John's gospel; as that is more full and satisfactory on the subject than the gospels of the other Evangelists.

the Christian religion follow of course: but there are many Deists, who, though they do not reject the whole account of the discourses, incidents and actions of Jesus, are yet only willing to admit it, as an heterogeneous mixture of truth and fiction; and, consequently, according to whom, the character of Jesus must have been, in part, taken from life, and, in part, from imagination.

For a moment, allowing this supposition, how are we to draw the line where the truth ends and the falsehood begins? All the discourses and actions of Jesus, which are recorded in the gospels, are intimately cemented together;—not by a connection of place, or by a continued chain of subordinate causation,—but by a certain peculiarity of character; which cannot escape the notice of the dilligent examiner; but which hardly admits of a definition, through the imperfections of language.*

---

* This peculiarity of character, is a good deal connected with the impressiveness, the majesty, and, at the same time, the genuine, unaffected simplicity of the manner; (on which I have spoken more at large in the next chapter;) but this is not all; and language is as inadequate to catch all the fleeting and intermingling tints and combinations of sensation, as it is to delineate all the tints and combinations of nature's ever-varying forms.—On it's inadequacy, as it relates to picturesque description, a subject which has lately been so much in fashion, I will say a few words.

By this peculiarity they are, if I may so express it, so completely identified with themselves, and with each other, that

---

Nature is characterised by diversity. In every landscape or view, with which she is adorned, though there may be a general cast of resemblance, yet there is always a great variety in the colouring—in the intermixture of light and shade—in the forms of particular objects, and their several combinations. But try to transfuse an exact likeness of these things into the artificial net-work of language; and you will soon discover that the terms of taste are not sufficiently copious or precise to express all the diversified sensations of beauty; and that the vocabulary of admiration is so jejune, that it is soon worn thread-bare.—Even the picturesque descriptions of Mrs. Radcliffe, though combined with all the exquisite taste of genius, and mellowed by the blush of sentiment, soon tire upon the ear and pall upon the sense.

In language, we may paint the general forms of rocks, woods, rivers, mountains and vallies, precipices, cataracts and torrents, and may group these several objects together, so as to give a faint resemblance of Nature's scenes; but it is impossible to hit, as it were, that versatility of touch, which she every where employs; and which prevents the forms of any two objects, however similar, from being the same. Hence we are soon wearied with that monotonous uniformity, which pervades the descriptions of picturesque travellers; though we should have experienced neither languor nor satiety in viewing the original scenes. In nature, every thing is infinitely diversified; but the variety of her dresses, her shapes, her combinations eludes the most subtle machinations of the genius of language.

In language, we have no other means of characterising the individuals of a species of objects, than by the use of epithets.—But the stock of epithets,—I do not mean, of those vacant sounds, which are used merely for the purpose of harmonising periods (a purpose, to which they are so copiously applied by modern writers), but of those epithets, which have a definite signification, and which excite distinct ideas, the stock is scanty indeed; and very inadequate to shew that particularity and, as it were,

it is impossible to mark the separation between the genuine and the fictitious history. If we allow the discourses of Jesus to be genuine, and yet his miracles to be false, we shall not escape the greatest embarrassment. For the discourses assert the miracles; and the miracles confirm the discourses. Take away the genuineness of the one, and you destroy the genuineness of the other. We must either allow, that the discourses and the miracles are both genuine, or both fictitious. If we adopt the latter supposition, we shall still be involved in those inconsistencies which I have mentioned above.

Again—if we suppose that the discourses of Jesus are a mixture of truth and fiction, of what Jesus really spoke, and what the Evangelists imagined; still it will be impossible to distinguish where the first ends, and the last begins: for, in all the numerous discourses which the Evangelists have ascribed to Jesus, there is, without

---

individuality, which is Nature's impress on every one of her works. By epithets, we can express only very general ideas of magnitude, of form and colour; but we can specify only a very slender portion of that variety of magnitudes, of forms and tints which *An Unseen but Well-known Hand* has scattered, with a sort of careless profusion through the whole expanse of creation.

an identity of sense or of expression, an identity of manner, of style and character. No man, of the least acuteness, can read the gospels without being convinced of this. But this identity of manner, of style and character, in the discourses, seems almost impossible to be reconciled with the supposition of their being a combination of truth and fiction; for falsehood never could have been patched upon truth, and particularly by different hands, and in such a variety of instances, without the point of their conjunction being very perceptible. A modern architect, might, with more probability of success, attempt to restore the remains of an ancient pile of Grecian simplicity, or of Gothic exuberance,* so

---

* It is surprising how the artists of the middle ages could communicate such lightness to such massy fabrics;—how they could insinuate that airy, wavering grace, which is seen in their immense ramifications of stone, which, growing from massy columnar trunks, form a shady, solemn avenue from one part to another of their religious buildings! How did they turn their beautiful arches and raise their heaven-shooting spires? In every thing else, they seem to have been deficient in the first principles of taste; but in architecture they rivalled the excellence of Greece; if not in symmetry of proportions, at least in grandeur of design, in strength of execution, in fertility of invention, and in variety of decoration. The reason seems to be, that, in architecture, they followed nature, and looked into nature's book, for bold and masterly conceptions; in architecture, they disclaimed all priestcraft or prescription—while, in every thing else, they were the stupid slaves of bigotry and superstition.

that the most diligent and curious observer could not discern the difference between the old work and the new.

The features of truth, can seldom be brought into such an intimate, and, as it were, impalpable, and invincible union with those of falsehood, as that the latter shall be entirely concealed. And yet this extreme probability must have happened, on the supposition—that the discourses of Jesus are a mass of truth and fiction.

  The Ancient Goths used to worship the Deity in groves and woods; and, perhaps, sometimes in those immense caverns, which are occasionally formed by nature among the rocks. When, in the progress of civilization, they left their woods and caves, and began to erect artificial churches —they imitated in stone, the shade, ramifications and solemnity of their woods, groves and caves. The doors, or arches, which lead to their places of worship, they decorated with a profusion of foliage and tendrils; which, with a sort of negligent wildness spread over the way.—This was either intended to represent the entrance to a cavern, about which are scattered a profusion of shrubs, bines or wildflowers; or the opening into a wood, formed by the opposite trees, intertwining with each other.
  The great west entrance into Litchfield cathedral is remarkable beautiful; in the middle arises the trunk of a tree, exactly delineated; and which, by an expansion of it's branches, on each side, forms a passage through two arches;—whence the whole avenue of columns, with their spreading ramifications towards each other, and along the roof, forms a perspective, which stays attention by it's grandeur and it's beauty.

Allowing the genuineness of the discourses, the truth of the miracles is a necessary deduction. In the discourses, there is a frequent assumption of miraculous powers, and a presumption of their notoriety. On these powers, Jesus solely and exclusively rests the truth of his mission. How would any person, of superior good sense and discernment, as even the enemies to Jesus must allow him to have been, have falsely arrogated the possession of such powers? Would he have rested his whole claim to veracity on a groundless assertion? Would he have disgraced himself by a falsehood, of which, every peasant in Israel could have convicted him?

It will be no easy matter to solve these difficulties, which I have stated, without allowing that Jesus delivered those discourses which the Evangelists have ascribed to him; and wrought those miracles, with which they are so frequently associated.

A PICTURE OF
CHRISTIAN PHILOSOPHY.

Confiderations on the marks of energy and authority that characterifed the manner of Jefus; and, of which, the features are accurately preferved in the narrative of the Evangelifts.

St. Mathew tells us (vii. 28.) that when Jefus had finifhed his fermon on the mount—" the people were aftonifhed at his doctrine; for he taught them as one having authority, and not as the Scribes."

The authoritative manner of Jefus, is diftinctly feen through the whole of the Sermon. He appears rather like a king pronouncing his decrees, and invefted with power to enforce their obfervance, than as an humble peafant, without friends or power. The contraft, between the manner of the speaker and his circumstances, is very remarkable; and is a strong proof, that he was no impostor.

Imposture is usually obsequious and insinuating when in weakness; presumptuous and overbearing when in power. In the former state it flatters and caresses the the passions of others; in the latter it gratifies it's own.

Now,—were Jesus an impostor, he must have possessed a degree of arrogance, unusual even to such men; and he must have attained the very difficult art of giving it that air which commands attention and respect, rather than that which, particularly when assumed in circumstances of inferiority and indigence, provokes aversion and disdain.

Emotions of respect, seldom fail to be excited by that genuine authority, of which, an inward consciousness appears in the outward aspect; while contempt is the usual consequence of a supercilious temerity; which blusters, and apes the gesture of strength, to disguise it's impotence.

Genuine authority, whenever it is visible in the manner, soon transfuses it's influence into the breasts of the beholder; it is formed to excite mingled sensations of affection, of esteem and reverence; while assumed and factitious authority, which is justly named arrogance, is calculated to produce no other emotions than those of contempt and ridicule.

Genuine authority, often possesses a force greater than that of physical power;* and the former, by a mere look or gesture, will, sometimes, counteract the strength of the latter—or, at least for a moment, palsy it's action.

Cæsar seems to have thought his power weak, till he could strengthen it by the authority of Cicero. The usurper wisely discriminated between moral and physi-

---

* The true distinction between power and authority, as far as they are subjects of political consideration, is this.—

"Power is physical force; acts by mechanical impulsion, and operates on the will by the fears: but authority is rather a moral force; which rules at pleasure the voluntary powers, by it's fascinating sway over the affections and the heart." *See sermons to the* "*Friends of Peace.*" 12mo. Fol. 57. *White.*

cal force; he was therefore anxious to affociate the terror of his arms, with the respect which was attached to the virtue and the genius of Tully. Cicero, confidered abstractedly as an individual, was of no importance; but, the authority he had obtained, and of which the the influence was combined with his very name, gave a sanction to any cause and any party he espoused.

Louis the XVI. the last and the best of the French monarchs, was never greater than in his misfortunes. Stripped of physical power, he seemed great by the power of authority. When summoned before the barbarous tribunal, which condemned him to an undeserved death, the majesty of authority had survived the wreck of the majesty of power. The manner of Louis, which was characterised by true greatness, seems to have inspired sensations of reverence, even in the breasts of his ferocious accusers.

But, without that splendor of eloquence, which in Tully captivated applause, or that splendor of station, which, in Louis, dazzled the beholder, even in it's setting ray, there seems to have been, in Jesus, an air of authority, at once impressive and venerable. This made him command respect in the garb of distress; and breathed around him a reverential awe of majesty, in circumstances, in which any common mortal would have been passed by with silent pity, or viewed with scoffing insolence.

The manner of Jesus, stamped with the genuine impress of an energy more than human, the Evangelists have delineated with the greatest simplicity, and without the least show of art.

In all the discourses, which the Evangelists have attributed to Jesus, there are evident traces of the dignity of the speaker.* His august and impressive mien, is

---

* A striking instance of the impressive and authoritative manner of Jesus, may be seen in his invective against the Pharisees, Matt. xxiii. The reader should peruse the whole chapter with attention. It shews the energy, the animation and the pathos which Jesus could combine on proper occasions.

In the viith and xth chapters of John, there are many delicate and lively traits of that peculiarly-impressive manner, which made the peasant of Galilee, " who had not where to lay his head," appear as " one having authority." The last discourses of Jesus to his disciples, detailed in John xiii. xiv. xv. xvi. are particularly deserving of attention. They are very descriptive of the manner of Jesus.—I particularly recommend what I have said on this subject to the calm and candid consideration of the author of the " Age of Reason" and his followers.

preserved without much fulness of colouring, but with great delicacy of tint and precision of outline, in the four pourtraits of Jesus, which have been drawn by the four Evangelists.

The same features are curiously kept, though in many different attitudes; and the same manner is observed, with inimitable skill, in a great diversity of incidents and sayings.

The manner of Jesus must certainly have been noticed by the Jews, as an extraordinary trait in his character, and must have been regarded with some emotions of reverence, or they would not have said of him, that " he spoke as one having authority." The Evangelists have, certainly, in their several histories, marked, with singular nicety, the meekness, yet the energy, the earnestness, the sincerity, and the air of conscious importance, which was observed in all that Jesus uttered. These combined qualities—the associates of genuine authority, commanded the respect of the beholder; and excited sensations, which artificial greatness in vain strives to emulate.

On this occasion, in perusing the Evangelical history, we cannot help being struck with the apparent incongruity between the grandeur of the authoritative manner of Jesus, and the meanness of his circumstances.

Whence could the Galilean peasant have devised the impressiveness of his manner? Whence could the saying of a poor, unfriended and houseless wanderer, have commanded as much attention as if they had come from one who had the sway of empires?

In the actual circumstances of Jesus (supposing him not to have possessed the divine powers which are ascribed to him), it must have been difficult, indeed impossible, for him to have preserved, in his whole deportment, in every word, in every gesture, all of which were exposed to a severe and malicious scrutiny—the air of majesty and the impression of authority.

If Jesus had been an impostor, and with no appendages of artificial grandeur, no recommendations of external power, his very assumption of the tones of authority, instead of exalting, must have degraded him in the eyes of the people. Inſtead of commanding attention, he would have provoked laughter.

The multitude are led entirely by appearances; and they never aſſociate ideas of reſpect with the image of penury and of wretchedneſs.

The great, and ſeemingly irreconcileable, diſparity between the manner of Chriſt and his condition, would certainly have excited contempt and ridicule, rather than thoſe emotions of ſeriouſneſs and awe, which genuine authority inſpires; if the meanneſs of his condition had not diſappeared in the real, not the affected dignity of his manner:

What he ſpoke commanded attention, becauſe it was ſpoken with genuine dignity; and becauſe the marks of a ſuperior energy were ſeen tranſlucent in Jeſus, through the veil of humiliating indigence. It was this that made even the moſt inveterate Jews, at times, liſten to him with ſilence and wonder. It was the manner of his ſayings and the air of authority, with which they were accompanied, that aſtoniſhed the Jews as much as their shrewdness. "Igneus est illis vigor, et *cælestis origo.*"

When the Pharisees and the chief priests sent officers to take Jesus, these very officers, struck with his manner, and with the dignified majesty, which attended whatever fell from his lips, were awed into emotions of reverence. They, therefore, returned to their employers without executing their commission: for " never," said they—" did man speak like this man." John vii. 46.

When a band of soldiers were sent to seize Jesus, in the garden of Gethsemane, John (xviii.) tells us, that Jesus " went forth and said unto them, whom seek ye?" " They answered him; Jesus of Nazareth." " Jesus saith unto them, *I am he.*" This simple but energetic declaration " *I am he,*" he seems to have made, " *as one having authority;*" and it marks the distinction between that authority which is genuine, and that which is assumed. For, the Evangelist says, that " when

Jesus had said unto them, *I am he, they went backward and fell to the ground.*"

A stronger or more natural instance of the influence of authority on the mind could not have been given. We see moral suspending the action of physical power.

The unbeliever will tell me, that this incident is a mere fiction of the Evangelist. I will only say, that supposing it a fiction, the historian was more than an ingenious man, so well to adapt the incident to the character, and the character to the incident.

But I can, by no means, think that such an incident would have been related, or even thought of, if it had not taken place. Was an historian so unlettered, and so little acquainted with the agency of metaphysical properties, likely to imagine, that the simple enunciation of Jesus, by the mere impalpable and spiritual force of authority, without a particle of physical power, should make a band of disciplined troops drop their arms and fall prostrate on the earth

This impreſſion is in perfect conſiſtency with the characteriſtic energy, which the four Eaangeliſts have with the moſt perfect harmony, appropriated to the manner of Jeſus; but it by no means leads to the concluſion that their relations are fabulous.

The manner of Jeſus, as it is delineated by the Evangeliſts, is uniformly the ſame;—impreſſive and authoritative through the whole recorded period of his miniſtry. Mean in his circumſtances, there are no meanneſſes, no littleneſſes in his manner. His ſeriouſneſs never dwindles into jocoſeneſs; or contracts into churliſhneſs; his earneſtneſs is never forſaken for levity; and his ſincerity is too manifeſt, too palpable even, for a moment, to excite diſtruſt.

As he draws to the cloſing ſcene of his ſufferings, his manner ſo artleſsly pourtrayed, in the ſimple narrative of the Evangeliſts, rather increaſes than decreaſes in it's dignity; his laſt diſcourſes, are, if any thing, more impreſſive and authoritative than any, which he had before delivered.* What he ſet out with being,

---

* Conſult the Goſpel of St. John, vii. x. xiii. xiv. xv. xvi.

he continued to be; and in his character, as it is represented by the Evangelists, there is not a single inconsistent or discordant trait, which can lead us to suspect the truth of the historians, or the accuracy of the likeness.

A PICTURE OF
CHRISTIAN PHILOSOPHY.

Remarks on the Christian miracles.

IT is too common for man to make the display of his power the only motive to it's exercise: but the Deity does not affect ostentatious greatness; benevolence directs all his operations. The miracles of our Saviour, resemble the agency of divine wisdom, in the course of nature; they are not a vain and idle display of power; they combine goodness with greatness, vastness of might with copiousness of beneficence.*

---

* There are but two miracles recorded of our Saviour, which do not bear the palpable marks of benevolence;—the destruction of the swine and of the fig tree. That Jesus should mingle two miracles of destruction, with his numberless miracles of mercy, is not remarkable; if we consider the useful inferences that are to be drawn from them. The mira-

Now, had the miraculous energies, which are ascribed to Jesus, existed only in the imagination of the historians, it is more than probable that the miracles, which they would have imputed to him, would have differed, materially, from those which the Evangelists have recorded. Originating from the invention of man, they would have proved, like the spurious wonders of Pythagoras or of Apollonius Thyaneus, their own refutation. Their inutility, their absurdity or their ostentation would have inevitably convicted them of falshood.

When men give themselves up to the invention of the marvellous, they soon stumble into extravagancies and inconsistencies. It is hardly possible for falshood, so closely to counterfeit the language of truth, as ingeniously to assimilate the features of fraud to the countenance of honesty, as not to leave the least semblance of of deception.

---

cle of the swine, shews us the importance of the guidance of the Divine Providence, in our way through life; without which our own passions, which are the most potent emissaries of Satan, will be our ruin; and will hurry us, as the fiends hurried the swine, into Destruction.

The miracle of the fig tree teaches us, that God expects us to be *prepared* to obey the summons to eternity, *in season* and out of *season*,—in youth, manhood, and in age.

Supposing the Christian miracles the fabrications of imposture, it must be confessed, that the Evangelists have related a series of lies, with all the artless simplicity, all the consistency, all the apparent ingenuousness, which we might expect in a narrative of facts, of which they were the eye-witnesses; and which they could not have a single motive to disguise.

In the relation of the Christian miracles, there is not a single indication of the least wish to guard against any objections that might be made to their authenticity. This shews the undaunted consciousness of truth. An impostor is usually, tremblingly anxious to anticipate objections; of which he betrays the force by his eagerness to repel it. A certain busy jealousy of caution to corroborate truth, always excites suspicion of falshood.

No suspicion of falshood, can possibly arise in the mind of any candid enquirer, from the unreserved, unguarded detail of the Christian miracles. They are told as plain matters of fact, of which, not the least doubt was entertained by the writers; and who, consequently, took no pains to provide antidotes against the distrust of their readers. Not haunted by the fears of imposture, they difdained to notice objections which were groundlefs; or to anfwer cavils which were vain.

Truth relies on it's native, inherent vigor; while falfhood, which is allied to cowardice, fortifies itfelf againft danger, by fuperfluous precautions; it lengthens the line of it's defence, and expofes it's impotence, by the bufy fcrupulofity of it's fears.

The miracles of Jefus bear, on the very face of them, an evidence of their truth; they are affociated with no circumftances which can excite the fufpicion of their being forgeries; and they are juft fuch miracles as we might fuppofe, from the moft ferious exercife of our natural reafon, would have been performed, for the purpofe of confirming any revelation, which the divine wifdom might vouchfafe to mankind.

The Chriftian miracles are fupported by two kinds of evidence, one internal, the other external. The external evidence has been amply treated of by other writers, and I do not wifh to make a book, by retailing arguments that frequent ufe has worn thread-bare; but I think, that the internal evidence has never yet been confidered with that attention which it deferves, or with that nicety of difcrimination of which it is fufceptible.

The ftrength of the internal evidence would be more clearly fhown, if any, the moft ingenious infidel would attempt to write the fictitious life of a perfon, faid to have been fent from heaven, on purpofe to promulgate a new religion, and to reveal the moft glorious and ufeful truths. Let the writer of this hiftory, which I am fuppofing, for the fake of argument, make the fubject of his narrative perform a variety of miracles; and let him try whether, with the utmoft labour, he could make them, in all refpects, in their characteriftic features, in their minute and incidental circumftances, half fo natural or fo apparently real as thofe recorded in the gofpel. Without any temerity of conjecture we might, I think, beforehand determine, that he, who fhould make this attempt, would not be able to produce a hiftory, which (without regarding it's proof from teftimony, from the circumftances of the times, or the records of contemporary hiftory,) would wear thofe artlefs and unvarnifhed features of genuinenefs, honefty and veracity, which are feen in every page of the memoirs which the Evangelifts have left us of **Jefus Chrift**.

There will always be, from the very structure of the human mind, certain nice and peculiar distinctions between forged and real history; which the writer of the former will overlook or will be unable to catch; but which will, at least, prevent his work from imposing on the generality of mankind.

In fabulous memoirs, either some relations will clash with some genuine circumstances of contemporary history, with some manners or usages of the same place, at the same period, or the writer will dwell so much on generalities, as to prove that he could not have been a contemporary of the times or the persons he describes, or an eye-witness of the facts he records; or else he will expatiate so long and largely on particulars—not distinct, appropriate, lively and interesting—but cold, superfluous, inapposite, incoherent—as evidently to betray an attempt to impose.

Nothing of this kind appears in the accounts of the Evangelists.—The historians of truth,—they have surmounted those difficulties, on which the historians of forgery would have stumbled; they have been betrayed into no inconsistencies, either in relation to former parts of their own narrative, or to the manners, cuftoms and laws of the country, where the facts occurred, or to the circumftances of contemporary hiftory; they have related occurrences in that unaffected, undifguifed manner, without too many or too few fpecialities, as eye-witneffes of the facts, and plain and honeft hiftorians naturally would do.—They fhew no defire to comprefs and curtail, or to dilate and embellifh; every thing they relate is told in a moft lively, natural and inartificial manner;—the narrative of the miracles, they atteft, if it be generally brief, is always circumftantial; and when copious, it never tires by tedioufnefs of digreffion or drynefs of detail. It's energy is not weakened by it's concifenefs; and it's fpirit is never evaporated in diffufenefs.

A PICTURE OF CHRISTIAN PHILOSOPHY.

Remarks on the miracle of the blind man restored to sight by Jesus; according to the account given by St. John ix.

I SHALL now proceed to corroborate and to exemplify several remarks, which have been made in the preceding pages, in a critical and circumstantial examination of the miracle of the restoration of a blind man to sight; which is related by St. John ix.

To this miracle, I humbly solicit the attention of those, who are disposed to imagine that there is no more credit due to the Christian miracles, than to the wildest fictions.

The miracle, I have selected for the subject of these observations, is related more in detail than any of the rest. It bears, at first sight, evident signs of it's authenticity; and which will be more apparent, if we contrast it with the most specious wonders of pagan history, or of popish artifice. It glows warm with the colouring of life and nature; and shows none of the awkward or incoherent combinations of a forgery. But let us proceed to the account of the miracle itself.—

" As Jesus passed by, he saw a man who was blind from his birth. And his disciples asked him, saying; Master, who did sin, this man, or his parents, that he was born blind?"

In this introduction, there is no trace of constraint or artifice. The relation opens with the most unaffected ease and air of sincerity. The first incident does not seem to have been feigned, to introduce what follows; and yet it does not inappositely coalesce with it.

To the question of his disciples, the Evangelist relates that Jesus answered, " Neither hath this man sinned nor his parents; but that the works of God should be

C

made manifest in him. *I must work the works of him that sent me, while it is day; the night cometh when no man can work.* AS LONG AS I AM IN THE WORLD, I AM THE LIGHT OF THE WORLD." Observe, in this reply, that characteristic confidence and energy, which marks almost all the sayings which the Evangelists have recorded of Jesus. The peculiarity of his manner, the discriminating air of his address is delineated, not with a coarse, but delicate hand, in the words which are printed in Italics and capitals.

It was usual with Jesus, to drop, as it were, incidentally, and to incorporate with apparently-extraneous matter, the most weighty sentences;—sentences which were uttered with impressive dignity; and which awaken the mind to the most serious reflections. "*The night cometh when no man can work!*" How much meaning, how much salutary and awful admonition is folded up in this last sentence!—" AS LONG AS I AM IN THE WORLD, I AM THE LIGHT OF THE WORLD." These words are another remarkable instance of Christ's manner, sententious and dignified. They bear the character of majesty, and show the unappalled consciousness of more than mortal dignity.

"When he had thus spoken, he spat on the ground and made clay of the spittle; and he anointed the eyes of the blind man with the clay, And he said unto him; go, wash in the pool of Siloam. He went his way therefore and washed, and came seeing."

This, by no means, looks like the act of an impostor; for such an one usually affects more mystery; and, at least, keeps his nostrums a secret. Jesus, certainly, could by his simple volition have effected the cure; but he seems to have resorted to this secondary means the more eminently to display his power.

The power of God is never more gloriously manifested, that when he produces great ends by feeble instruments. In the miracle which we are considering, common sense must have told the spectators, that the mixture of spittle with dirt, could not have restored sight to one born blind. But so simple and insignificant an application only served to shew, more forcibly, the divine energy that animated the physician.

Had this miracle not been genuine and real, but one which existed only in the imagination of the writer, who was desirous of imposing it on the credulity of the world, it seems probable, that he would have made the hero of his tale adopt a more complicated and mysterious mode of cure; and, at the same time, affect a greater degree of skill. It is likewise probable that the narrator, after having told us that the blind man " went and washed and came seeing," would have indulged himself in some expressions of panegyric, * on the wisdom or the benevolence of Jesus; but instead of this the Evangelist details a long conversation, which took place on the subject of the cure; and, at which, he seems to have been himself present. His account of it is so vivid, and the transitions in the dialogue so abrupt, and yet natural; as they usually are, on subjects which provoke minuteness of examination, and excite the impatience of contradiction. This will be visible even through the medium of a translation. †

---

* One strong proof of the truth of the gospel history is, that there is not a single line in it, which breathes even a whisper of adulation.—All is plain, unadorned narrative; facts occupy the place of eulogies.

† There are very few persons, who, though they may write other languages can think in any but their own. Much as they may endeavour, they can hardly help tinging a foreign language with the peculiarities of their vernacular tongue,

" The neighbours, therefore, and they which before had seen him that he was blind, said; Is not this he that

---

The Greek of the Evangelists, is tissued with Hebraisms; though they wrote in the first language, they thought in the last.—This, by the by, is an argument against those, who pretend that the gospels were written under the immediate and plenary influence of inspiration;—for, had the thoughts been inspired; the language, in which those thoughts are conveyed, must have been inspired likewise; for very few ideas (those alone excepted which represent sensible objects) can be communicated to the mind of another, but through the medium of words.

It may be said that the Almighty could convey to the mind of man even the most abstract notions, without the intermediate use of their ordinary signs.

It is certainly wrong to limit the power of God; but it is equally wrong to multiply miracles without necessity. This is to criminate his wisdom, and, in fact, to question his power, which is always the practical influence of his wisdom.

But it may be said, that the divine communications were imparted to the Evangelists through the medium of language; but that this language was not the Greek but the Hebrew.—To this, we must reply, that Providence always takes the shortest method to accomplish his designs; and that it is therefore more natural to suppose, that had the history of the Evangelists been written under the plenary energy of immediate inspiration, the narrative would have been transmitted to their minds, through the medium of the language *in which it was to be written*; that the historian might not be under the necessity of translating into corrupt Greek, what was inspired in pure Hebrew. If inspiration were necessary to the Evangelists, it was as necessary that the language they wrote in should be inspired, as well as the thoughts; in order to prevent those inaccuracies, which would otherwise necessarily occur, in translating thoughts out of a vernacular into a foreign idiom.

sat and begged? Some said; This is him: others said; He is like him: but he said; I am he!"

There seems, to me, to be no occasion whatever for supposing, that the historical parts either of the Old or New Testament were indited under a divine and uncontroulable influence.

Had the Evangelists such short memories, that they could not speak truth without the aid of inspiration? Were they not competent to give a faithful narrative of transactions, which had passed either before their own eyes or the eyes of their contemporaries? Like honest historians, could they not conscientiously relate what they had seen and heard? We pay them a poor compliment by the contrary supposition.—There are, certainly, some few variations in the memoirs of the Evangelists, which, though they *rather confirm than invalidate their authority, considering them as mere human compositions*, are yet totally irreconcileable with the belief of *their full and unconditional inspiration.*

The universal and unconditional inspiration of the Scriptures cannot be maintained; but the inspiration of the prophetic parts, particularly of those which relate to the coming of the Messiah, and the dispersion of the Jews, is capable of demonstrative proof. At this post let us make our stand against all assailants.

Whether the narrative of the Evangelists be inspired or not, it cannot be doubted by any, who are acquainted with both Greek and Hebrew, or who have perused the learned volumes of Michaelis, that the Greek of the Evangelists is cast in the mould of the Hebrew idiom. Hence arises the difficulty of affixing a precise and definite meaning to many passages in the sacred volume; and hence we ought, in many cases, where the native simplicity of the Greek is disguised under the veil of Eastern metaphor, to allow some latitude of interpretation; and, not always, to limit the sense, within the strict and literal acceptation of the words. I am, by no means, for affixing a mystical construction *to any passages* in Scripture; but such an one as should occasionally modify, restrain or amplify the literal sense, so *as to suit the Eastern idiom,—in which the writers thought, and in which their meaning, wherever it is dubious, must, of course, be sought.*

How natural is all this! It has the animation of life, and the simplicity of truth. The curiosity of the spectators was a good deal excited by the miracle, which had been performed; but yet it was so extraordinary an one, that their minds fluctuated, as might have been expected, between conviction and distrust. "Some said, This is he; others said, This is like him;" but the poor man, as if jealous of the reputation of the miracle, and proud of the privilege of sight, exclaims—" *I am he.*"

" Therefore, said they unto him; how were thine eyes opened?" To this question he answers, " A man that is called Jesus, made clay and anointed mine eyes; and said unto me; Go to the pool of Siloam and wash; and I went and washed, and I received sight. Then said they unto him; Where is he?" (This question shews the emotion of impatient curiosity, turning from the object to the author of the miracle.) " He said, I know not."

The person who had been blind was now brought before the Pharisees. We are first told that it was the Sabbath day, when Jesus made the clay and opened his eyes. "Then again the Pharisees also asked him, how he had received his sight. He said unto them; He put clay upon mine eyes; and I washed and do see. Then they called the parents of him that had received his sight."

A modern Skeptic could hardly have questioned the validity of any miracle more acutely than the Pharisees did, on this occasion; and in the true spirit of some modern unbelievers, when they could not invalidate the fact, they sought for a confutation in obloquy and passion.

"Is this your son, whom ye say was born blind? how then doth he now see?" The Pharisees, perhaps, expected that the parents of the poor man, intimidated at the sternness of their manner, would either confess their ignorance of the matter, or would give such answers to their questions, as should gratify their wishes, by shaking the credibility of the fact. The answer, however, which the parents returned, though cautious, was by no means evasive.

"We know," said they, "that this is our son, and that he was born blind; but by what means he now seeth we know not; he is of age; ask him; he shall speak for himself." The Evangelist here speaks with all the particularity of an eye-witness, in the scene he describes; and how little does what he has here said favour of a forgery!

The Pharisees, baffled in their purpose, and hardly knowing how to get rid of the impression, which the miracle had made, again called for the person who had received his sight; and said unto him; " Give God the praise; we know that this man is a sinner." Observe the art of the Pharisees; unable to disprove the fact they endeavour to set aside the inferrence, and to silence the voice of truth by dogmatical assertion. " WE KNOW *that this man is a sinner.*"

How natural is the reply to this speech! such as the event certainly prompted; but such, as if the miracle had been a fiction of fancy, was by no means, likely to have been invented. " He answered and said; Whether he be a sinner or no, I know not; one thing I know, that whereas I was blind, now I see." He does not, till he is further provoked, *openly deny* the assertion of the Pharisees, that Jesus was a sinner; but he artfully, though silently, refutes it, by referring them to the miracle.

The Pharisees, who seem to have been incensed by the poor man's answer, proceed to bluster and to browbeat him, as some counsellors do a witness, whom they want to make to deny or recant the truth. They say unto him, in the short and abrupt interrogatories of passion; "How did he to thee? How opened he thine eyes?"

Here the Evangelist, in a measure, makes us spectators in the scene; and delineates, in a very characteristic manner, the impatience and the fury of the Pharisees.

The poor man, stimulated by the vehemence of his adversaries, grows, in his turn, warmer in his manner; and answers their scoffs by a dry but very sarcastic insinuation. "I have told you," said he, "already and ye did not hear; wherefore would ye hear it again? *Will ye also be his disciples?*"

"Then they reviled him and said; Thou art his disciple; but we are Moses's disciples. We know that God fpake unto Mofes; as for this fellow, we know not whence he is."

The poor man, now, inftigated by repeated contradiction, and warmed with emotions of gratitude towards his benefactor, proceeds to defend him againſt the contemptuous language of his accuſers. He ſays; "Why, herein is a marvellous thing, that ye know not from whence he is, and yet he hath opened mine eyes. Now we know that God heareth not ſinners; but, if any man be a worſhiper of God, him he heareth. Since the world began, was it not heard that any man opened the eyes of one that was born blind. If this man were not of God, he could do nothing."

The rage of the Phariſees could no longer be reſtrained; they ſaid unto him; "Thou waſt altogether born in ſins, and doſt thou teach us? And they caſt him out."

Had this miracle been a mere fiction of the hiſtorian; we cannot well ſuppoſe that he would have inſerted the ſubſequent dialogue, which is a curious and ſhrewd inveſtigation of the fact, by the ſpirit of ſkepticiſm; and which has not the least appearance of an ideal fabrication; but which, as far as internal evidence can go, proves the reality of the miracle, which it contests. In the course of the dialogue, the gradations of passion are marked with great vivacity, in the quickness of the transitions, and the abruptness of the dispute; and the whole, instead of being the combination of ingenious artifice, seems the easy, natural and unaffected relation of one, who had seen and heard all that he relates.

In the poor sufferer, who had received his sight, we behold reiterated obloquy rousing timidity into boldness; and animating truth from an indirect and trembling confession, into an open and manly avowal;—in the Pharisees, we see cunning, mortified into rage; and baffled falshood, ending in angry violence. "They cast him out."

The narrative of false miracles is commonly it's own confutation; and, if this miracle be a fictitious one, we must allow that the unlettered Evangelist excelled in the delicate refinements of fraud; and that he possessed the singular talent of habiting the guilt of fraudulent imposture—not in specious or wanton ornaments—but in the more winning, becaufe genuine, attire of fimplicity and truth. *

Would to God! that any thing which I have faid on this miracle, could imprefs any one with fuch a conviction of it's reality, as that it might remove the film of infidelity from his intellectual fight, and pour into it the light of immortality!

---

* The account of the miracle, does not conclude with the altercation between the perfon who had received his fight and the Pharifees. The Evangelift proceeds to relate it's moral influence on him on whom it had been wrought. Jefus having heard of his treatment by the Pharifees, faid unto him—" Doft thou believe on the Son of God?"—" And he faid, Lord, I believe. And he worfhiped him. And Jefus faid, for judgment I am come into this world; that they which fee not might fee, and that they which fee might be made blind." Obferve the authoritative manner of Jefus.

A PICTURE OF
CHRISTIAN PHILOSOPHY.

The character of Jesus illustrated.

THE character of individuals may be usually identified with the influence of early impressions. Those impressions, made at a time when the susceptibility of excitement is the greatest, and when the sensations possess a peculiar vivacity, commonly constitute the basis of character. They communicate to the mind and the affections their discriminating features. In infancy, how frequently do we imbibe the seeds of those sympathies, which, invisibly, influence the happiness or the misery of our future lives!!! *

---

* That peculiar bent of mind, which discriminates individuals through life, and which, when it displays itself, with a predominating

From the circumstances, in which Jesus appears to have been placed in early life, we might suppose, that a

---

vigor, in any branch of art or science, is commonly called Genius, is probably derived from early sympathies; and which often take place so early that it is impossible to trace them to their original source. Sir Joshua Reynolds, as we are informed by Johnson, in his life of Cowley, imbibed the first fondness for his favourite art, from the perusal of Richardson's treatise on painting.

Chatterton, probably derived his partiality for antiquities, from having been taught his letters from some illumined leaves of an old missal.

The strange antipathies, hallucinations, or false and preposterous combinations of ideas, which we may frequently observe among our fellow-creatures, seem likewise, for the most part, to be the result of early association. When sensations of a very lively nature have once been felt in the sensorium, their influence is likely to remain; and reason often in vain attempts to abate it. In this case, reason is usually found a feeble adversary to sensation. In childhood, the power of sensation is stronger than that of reason; but as reason gradually unfolds it's energies, the power of sensation becomes less, that of reason greater;—except in those particular instances, in which sensation, aided by the adventitious force of some extraordinary, incidental impressions, gains an ascendant over the reason; from which the latter can never, afterwards, accomplish it's deliverance. Thus, when young people have been frightened, through the folly of their mothers or their nurses, by the terrific tales of apparitions, and have, by this means, had the sensation of fear powerfully excited, they can seldom, as they grow up, entirely break the spell of these terrible illusions.—The sensation of terror, strong and over-bearing, palsies the exertions of the reason; and produces, under particular circumstances, a deplorable state of mental imbecility; which precludes the power of counteracting the hallucinations of the fancy, by the energy of intellect. How does fancy make fools of us all!! Even the aspiring genius of philosophy has been sometimes crushed into cowardice by it's vain and illusory shadows!

very different character would have been formed, from that represented by the Evangelists. The parents of

---

We are liable to be ruled by the influence of incidents or impressions, which we have forgotten; or, in other words, sensations are subject to revival by association, when the causes which first produced them are remembered no longer. Who then can calculate the power of incidental impressions? and how studious ought those, who have the care of children, to be, that no impressions be made on their minds, which, as the very sagacious author of Zoonomia has observed, may bias their affections or mislead their judgments to the ends of their lives. See Zoonom. ii. 386. Education, as far as it respects the formation of habits, cannot be begun too early.—Habits which beget peevish and unsocial tempers, and which tend to moral depravity, by being associated with malevolence, are probably often formed, by the mismanagement of mothers and nurses, in the first period of childhood. At that period, the faculty of association is most alive and vigorous; and which, according to it's peculiar determination, usually influences the temper and the character of man to the last of his days.

How many useful lessons might the preceptors of youth learn from meditating deeply on the power and influence of early associations!—How subservient might they render them to the cause of science and of benevolence!—The evil effects of early impressions are readily seen; but a wise system of education would counteract the bad and promote the good. We should be particularly solicitous to engraft into the heart, while it is yet incorrupt and innocent, habits of benevolence; and which might readily be effected, by taking advantage of little incidents and casual occurrences, to connect the practice of benevolence with the vivacity of pleasurable sensation; and which would be subject to revival by association, when the incidents, which first excited it, were forgotten. Were pleasurable feelings connected with the idea of benevolence, at a very early period, and before the love of sensual or selfish pleasure had made any very deep impression on the heart, so as to counteract the growth of the amia-

Jesus were poor, and lived in obscurity; gaining their livelihood by their humble industry. They therefore

---

sympathies, *the affections would receive a forceable and originally-virtuous bias; which the future intercourse with, or experience of the ordinary selfishness of mankind might modify, but would never destroy.*

The reader will excuse me, if I add another remark to this long note; of which, I hope the length will be excused, from it's relation to a most important, nay, *the* most important topic of human enquiry;—The formation of the mind to science and to virtue.———I will add, then, careless of the censure, which the observation may bring upon me, from the trifling and the licentious, that if we wish to encourage the free expansion of the benevolent principle in children, we ought never to put a card into their hands.—Young people are brought up, with the notion that card-playing is a pretty, innocent recreation. They, therefore, at a very early period, learn to associate the idea of gaming with many ideas of pleasure; and not, as they ought, with sensations of shame, of pain and disappointment.—I hardly know any admonition which a parent ought more assiduously to instil into his child than this,—that all gaming is a species of robbery by delusion, that it engenders fraud and ends in misery. Even the less species of gaming, which are deemed so perfectly harmless, and so nicely adapted to fill up the yawning vacancies of fatuity,—even these lead directly to a fatal depravation of the moral principle, by extinguishing the benevolent affections.—I never knew a confirmed and habitual card-player, who had not a callous and unfeeling heart. It is indeed impossible for any one long to retain the general glow of one benevolent sympathy, who habitually associates, like the inveterate card-player, sensations of triumph and of pleasure, with the vexations and disappointment of others. Even the least and most innocuous species of gaming have a fatal tendency to imbue, with the taste of pleasure, the emotions of malevolence; and, indeed, we cannot long be partakers in a single amusement, into which one drop of the spirit of gaming has been infused, without it's diminishing the power of that susceptibility of catch-

D

could not afford to give him what among the Jews was called a learned education. He was, probably, brought up to the profession of his father; and, supposing him no more than an ordinary mortal, the only means he had of acquiring that knowledge, which was requisite to empower him to subvert the religious institutions of his own country, and of the world, and to become the founder of a new and spiritual worship, of a house of prayer for all nations, were, by attending the synagogue, and the solemn feasts at Jerusalem.

The whole literature of the Jews consisted of one book—the Law and the Prophets, with the comments and traditions of the Scribes and Pharisees. These were

---

ing the sensations of others, and of mingling them with our own; from which sympathy flows, and by which benevolence is excited.—Must not then the higher and more criminal species of gaming tend, with a direct and accelerated influence, to chill the benevolence of the heart, and to fear the sense of integrity of conduct? Does not the spirit of gaming, rankling in the heart, and gradually, but rapidly, undermining all within, infallibly create the cruel and designing villain? Does he not soon learn to plunder the unwary without shame, and even to triumph in proportion to the misery and indigence he produces? Hear this! ye heroes and heroines of Faro. Would to God, it could raise one blush on your livid cheeks, or one emotion of remorse in your callous hearts!!!

the only sources of wisdom, to which he could have access; but from these, had Jesus not been under a divine influence, imparting wisdom from above, he must have been debarred by ignorance. For we gather from John vii. 15, 16. that he had received no literary instruction whatever. "How (said the Jews) knoweth this man letters, having never learned?" What learning he possessed was not an artificial acquisition. "My doctrine (said Jesus, in reply to the objection of the Jews,) is not mine, but his that sent me."

A child usually imbibes, at least, some portion of the prejudices of his parents, and of those among whom he is educated. The universal prejudices of the jews, at the time of the nativity of Jesus, are well known. Among these prejudices, one of the most predominant, was the expectation of a triumphant Messiah, a conceited opinion of their own, and a supercilious disdain of all other nations. These prejudices, instilled by his parents and acquaintance, would have flowed softly and almost insensibly into the bosom of Jesus. And, had he been only an impostor, it is more than probable that he would himself have been the dupe of those early preposfeſſions;* and certainly he would not have taken ſo direct a ſtep to defeat his own views, by oppoſing the

---

* When men are prejudiced againſt truth, no proofs, even amounting to demonſtration, are ſufficient to convince them of it. Blinded by the prepoſſeſſions of error, they ſee every argument that is advanced through a falſe medium. The Phariſees, though they would gladly have received the Meſſiah, if he had appeared in the form and manner, in which their prejudices had anticipated his coming; yet, notwithſtanding all the miraculous proofs of his divine miſſion, they turned from him with abhorrence and diſguſt, when they found that his appearance and his circumſtances did not agree with their former darling expectations.

If we enter on the inveſtigation of any two opinions, with the leaſt bias on either ſide, or with any partial wiſhes that the one may be falſe, the other true, we are almoſt ſure, and without knowing it, to be led into error. We give too much weight to the arguments on one ſide, too little to thoſe on the other. Thus it has often happened, that the ſuppoſed truths of philoſophers, have been no better than the abortion of infant prejudices. We muſt continue to be led aſtray by prepoſſeſſions, while, inſtead of ſeeking truth, for truth's ſake, we ſet up an idol of our own vanity in it's place; and endeavour to adjuſt the ſtandard of truth to the ever-varying beam of our affections.

All truth is of importance; but religious truth is moſt important; as the greateſt happineſs is connected with it.—The firſt impreſſions of religious truth are commonly made in childhood. If theſe impreſſions happen to be falſe or pernicious, they can ſeldom be removed, to make way for more ſalutary notions.—If we ſit down at an advanced period of life, to make up our minds on religious matters, and to adopt that mode of faith and worſhip which ſhall appear moſt agreeable to Scripture, ſcrutinized by candour and interpreted by reaſon, it is ten to one, but we are miſled by the imperceptible and treacherous influence of paſt aſſociations. Thus, religious opinions, even thoſe which may be ſaid to be formed by mature conſideration, are ſeldom untinctured with the prejudices of in-

favourite, the long and universally received notions of his countrymen. Had he aspired from ambitious or from personal views to counterfeit the Messiah, he would not have attempted to extirpate the prejudices of a whole people, but to turn them to account; he would have taken advantage of every circumstance, to maintain the character he assumed; and to make the popular opinion subservient to his temporal aggrandizement.

But, in the very commencement of his ministry, Jesus directly combated the bigoted attachments, the

---

fancy.—This ought to teach us to treat the opinions of others without asperity, to advance our own with modesty, and to defend them without bigotry. Of the many modes of faith, which exist among Christians, one only can be right; and it is arrogance and impiety in any man to say that his is *that one*; and that, consequently, all others are erroneous. In matters of religious opinion, no man is rashly to condemn his brother; for no man can advance beyond probability in the proof that his way is the right. But though I would encourage, in individuals, charity, forbearance, and mildness in judging of the religious tenets of others; yet I would, by no means, recommend a cold, languid and lifeless indifference with respect to the complexion of their own. On the contrary, I earnestly exhort every one to embrace with warmth, but without acrimony,—with steadiness, but without perverseness, that mode of faith and worship which, from the best and most unprejudiced enquiry he can make, he conscientiously believes the right; and then he may securely rely that God will pardon him, if he be in the wrong. A just and merciful judge will, we may be convinced, never punish the adoption of opinions that were false, when it was honestly supposed that they were *true*.

darling prepoffeffions of every Jew; and boldly oppofed his fingle and feeble arm, to ftem the current of thofe popular notions, which, at that time, rolled with a fierce impetuofity through the whole extent of Paleftine; and of which, he, himfelf, had he been no more than man, could hardly have fuftained the overwhelming force. What individual can refift the powerful influence of general fympathy?

When, therefore, Jefus fet up for the propagator of a new religion, he muft either have unlearned the prejudices, and totally erafed the impreffions of his early years; which, on the fuppofition of his mortality, is highly improbable; or we muft allow that he was exempted by the peculiar bleffing of the divine influence, from the force of thofe primary affociations, which, according to the ufual laws of action, affect the character and the conduct to the clofe of life.

Let us now look a little nearer into the character of Jefus, and inveftigate fome of it's peculiar and difcriminating excellencies.

In Jefus, we behold none of thofe fhowy and noify virtues, which dazzle vulgar eyes, and attract vulgar praise. In his character, there are none of those ornamental features, which are more subservient to ambition than to utility. There is neither in his actions nor his sentiments the least of parade. There is no fascinating splendour, to cheat the judgment into admiration. There is every thing truly great, without the least show of greatness. It is a character totally distinct from that proud and fiery impetuosity, which often passes for magnanimity; from that sullen apathy, which is sometimes mistaken for grandeur; from that undistinguishing and visionary zeal, which is the mimic of devotion; and from that affectation of purity, which usurps the name of holiness.

It is a character which is inimitable; while it seems rather below than above the level of human imitation. The passive virtues are it's most conspicuous features; and these, however they may be depreciated by common minds, or however easy of attainment they may be accounted, are, in truth, more difficult to be acquired, and more productive of happiness, than the energies of a busy and a turbulent disposition.

But, if the character of Jesus be discriminated by the loveliest features of gentleness, meekness and forbearance, patience, humility and resignation; still it is marked with more energetic qualities; by a benevolence, which is ever awake to the touch of sympathy, which is ever vigorously employed in dissipating misery. If he be adorned by a mildness that resents no insult and retaliates no injury, he, at the same time, displays a spirit ardent in opposing error and combating wickedness.

Jesus begins his celebrated sermon on the mount, by bestowing the tribute of eternal blessedness on those unostentatious qualities, and retired graces, which least excite the envy or the admiration of the world. It is observable, that he commends those affections and virtues most, by which he was himself most eminently distinguished. He was always the pattern of his own lessons. He taught what he practiced; and he practiced what he taught. He was poor in spirit; he was meek, merciful and pure in heart.

The more we examine the blamelessness of his life, and the spirit of his doctrine, the more we shall be convinced that, Jesus was thoroughly acquainted with the mind and affections; and with the efficient causes of human happiness or misery. He knew that the great sum of the afflictions of life was occasioned by turbulence, vindictiveness and malignity of disposition. Hence all public and private strife; the seeds of animosity between individuals and nations. On this account, Jesus laid so much stress upon the passive virtues—on the silent kindness of the heart. Were meekness, gentleness and forbearance universal, the sword might rest in it's scabbard—every kingdom and every house would be a temple of peace.

The fiery spirit of revenge is most predominant, in that state of human nature, which is farthest removed from the knowledge of the Deity and from religious purity. The nearer approaches which man makes to the divine perfections, the more will this savage passion be abated. But though revenge be a passion utterly irreconcileable with the spirit of pure religion, still the complete suppression of it, is utterly impossible to man without the divine assistance. For man, being made, exquisitely sensible to pleasure and to pain, has naturally a desire for the first, and an aversion for the last. Hence, he cannot help associating some idea of malevolence with the image of those, who wilfully inflict painful sensations. The passion of hate begins, however faintly, to ferment the moment an injury is felt; and, even in the gentleft of human bofoms, there is fome tranfient interval of paffion, before the religious fentiments or benevolent fympathies can check the angry effervefcence.

Every phyfical fenfation of pain, is accompanied with a wifh to remove it; and where is it fo natural to wifh to remove it, as to the caufe which occafioned it?—Hence the defire of reverberating pain and retaliating injuries. A revenge of this kind, which is rather of a phyfical than of a moral nature, would ceafe with the fenfations that produced it. But revenge, we know, often rankles in the heart, long after the caufe which firft excited it has ceafed to exert any painful influence. The fentiment of refentment is cherifhed by malignant reflections, when it's firft effervefcence has fubfided; and is combined with many affociated ideas of honour or of pleafure, till cruelty almoft becomes a paftime.

How much might we diminifh the fum of human mifery, if we could, in fome meafure, reverfe the common order of human fympathies, and teach children univerfally to affociate the idea of honour with forbearance, and of pleafure with forgivenefs!!! How much rancour and bloodshed might, by this means, be prevented!!! The happiness of individuals, is, I am inclined to believe, always in a direct ratio with their benevolent sympathies;—the happiness of mankind, considered in the aggregate, evidently is.

Of all the persons recorded in history, Jesus seems the only one who ever obtained a complete triumph over the passion of resentment; and, in whose bosom, it was totally absorbed in the opposite passion of love. This love, he demonstrated by an uniform meekness and forbearance; by the happiness he diffused while he lived and when he died. He endured with patience, and without the least acrimony, persecution, scorn and insult; he never returned railing for railing; but, contrarywise, blessing. He exhibited that poorness of spirit, which is the highest degree of magnanimity; in as much as a victory over the angry passions, and the indignant feelings that rage for vent in the bosom, is the most difficult and most glorious of atchievements. The conqueror of Darius and of Persia was ruled, like a weak woman, by the gust of his resentments. But he, who triumphed over the cross, was signalized by a greater atchievement than the subjugation of kings, or the subversion of empires;—by the mastery of himself! He never performed any action, that, in the least, indicated resentment; he never uttered a word of anger or a taunt of bitterness.

Such was the meekness and forbearance of him, who is, by a beautiful emblem of innocence, called—the Lamb of God. Of this temper and carriage he set us the example; because he knew that it would most effectually promote our happiness here; and fit us for an intercourse with the blessed spirits hereafter; who dwell in the mansions of peace, where turbulence and malignity can never enter.

Jesus laid the utmost stress, in most of his discourses, on the importance of the placid and the benevolent affections; and, probably, from their being the essential characteristics of that state of future happiness, to which the good Christian hopes for a passage through the grave. It is the opinion of the immortal Hartley, that the associations or sympathies, we contract on earth, will accompany us into a future state. If this be true, and it is certainly no unscriptural doctrine, but apparently confirmed by the general *tendency* of the discourses of

Jesus, of what vast consequence is it to us, to cherish the benevolent sympathies, and to indulge all the kind affections!!! How studiously ought parents to labour, to instil them into their children, that they may grow up with them, and, after this life, expand into immortal happiness! How earnestly ought we to check the progress of all malevolent sensations! How anxious should we be to avoid associating any ideas of pleasure with the sight of misery, with the infliction of pain, or with any act of inhumanity! The malignant passions are, even here, the source of the acutest misery, to those who unfortunately indulge them; and on the supposition, * I

---

* The Scriptures give us reason to expect a resurrection of the individual. What constitutes individuality is the consciousness of identity. Our resurrection, or return to life, will not be complete, unless the consciousness, which constitutes the individuality of our present being, be annexed to our future. That this consciousness be complete, it is necessary that those associated sensorial motions and sympathies, which constitute what may be called our moral nature, here, should pass with us into another world. In this life, improveable faculties, particularly of affection and sympathy, are committed to us; and I think it probable, that our next stage of existence will, probably, be a state of improvement — Our Saviour has intimated to us, that, in heaven, there are many mansions. It is, therefore, highly probable, that, in these mansions, the condition and circumstances of existence will be purposely adapted to the former associated moral habits of the individual; and best suited to their farther expansion and improvement. Supposing man destined to an eternal exist-

have stated, they will prove a source of the most exquisite torment in another life. Thus, the associations,

---

ence, we cannot imagine, that the first moment he is made the citizen of another kingdom, he will become as wise or as virtuous as he is capable of being; or as he will ever be; and that he will thus continue stationary, at one point, through all the revolutions of infinite time. It is a far more reasonable and probable conjecture, that, in a future life, individuals will begin where they left off in this;—that they will still possess improveable faculties, but to which, a greater vigor will be communicated, in proportion to the greater objects, about which they will be occupied; and the wider sphere of existence, which they will embrace.

As individuals are to carry with them into other mansions their former associations and sympathies, the benevolent and the malevolent, or the good and the wicked, must, after death, occupy very different states of being; the former will migrate to a state of comfort and happiness—the latter of torment and misery.

The benevolent, who have cherished and have exercised all the kind and tender affections, will hereafter find them a source of the most exquisite joy;—of a joy not mingled, as in this world, with bitterness, or soured by disgust. They will find objects suited to the expansion of every amiable sympathy, with which their hearts were ever warmed; and in proportion as the benevolent affections of the soul expand and multiply, by being placed in a scene more congenial to their nature,— in a scene where kindness, instead of being blasted by ingratitude, will meet with kindness, and love with love;—in the same proportion, must the stock of their individual happiness be augmented.

Far different will be the lot of the malevolent; who have associated ideas of pleasure with any acts of inhumanity; who have wilfully marred the fair prospects of others happiness, or contracted an insensibility to others misery! We may imagine that such persons will, in a future scene of being, be placed under such circumstances, and amid such relations, as that the want of benevolence shall be to them a source of exquisite torture and unutterable woe.

of this state not being dissolved in the next, the malignant will be punished by habitual and inalienable sensa-

---

The eternity of punishments for temporary offences, and committed by beings who are covered with frailties, seems difficult to be reconciled to that attribute of INFINITE MERCY, or *what with respect to an All-perfect Being, is the same thing* that attribute of INFINITE JUSTICE, which belongs to the Maker of the universe, and the Father of mankind. May we not therefore infer (I speak with deference to older and wiser theologicians), without derogating, IN THE LEAST, *from the truth of Scripture*, that those passages which describe future punishments as eternal, are to be figuratively construed; that they intend pains *of long — not of* **infinite duration**; —*vast — not irremediable or never-ceasing affliction!* The wisest and best legislators among men, have never considered punishment in any other light, than as conducive to moral amendment;—and is it not blasphemy against the divine attributes, to suppose that the All-wise, All-just, and All-merciful *will ever inflict punishment for it's own sake, and without any view to the good or the reformation of him on whom it is inflicted?* Let not our ignorance of the true Scripture idiom, and of Eastern phraseology, lead us to this climax of folly and presumption!!!

From a serious investigation of the Divine attributes, and a candid and rational interpretation of Scripture, we may infer that the punishment of the wicked, in another world, *is designed for, and will tend to, their amendment;*—and, consequently, that the malevolent will be gradually, though slowly, and by the experience of severe and excruciating misery, cured of their habits of malignity. The difficulty of eradicating habits, which have been long indulged, is universally acknowledged; and, in a future world, it is not improbable that this difficulty may be still more difficult. Thus, the punishment of the malignant, in another state of existence, tho' not eternal, *must necessarily be of long continuance;*—of a continuance so long as in the bold, unconditional and hyperbolical menace of the Eastern language, to merit *the name of the everlasting fire.* Their agonies will, probably, have a duration beyond the reach of our narrow notions of time;

tions of their own malignity. They will, in some measure, resemble the Devil, the real or allegorical element of evil; who is painted, in scripture, as continually going about, seeking whom he may devour; destitute of a single spark of one benevolent sympathy;—the image of pure, unmixed malignity!!! Could he have been more forcibly delineated, either to excite terror or abhorrence? But let us return to the contemplation of a more pleasing form.

Of genuine humility, Jesus was a striking example, in his whole deportment; in every gesture, every word, every action. His humility was not the affectation of that virtue, which is so often assumed in the world, to cover an intolerable pride. It was pure and unadulterated; not the show, but the substance of a lowly heart.

That the humility of Jesus was not a veil for arrogance, or for vanity, he gave the most lively instance, on the night before his crucifixion, in washing the feet

---

and will last till the consciousness of guilt has entirely vanished; and the soul, no longer it's own tormentor, expands to the pleasures of benevolence.

of his disciples. This act of humiliation he performed, as a lasting admonition against that pride of heart, which often makes man look with disdain on his brother-man.

There is nothing more ludicrous, in the eye of a contemplative philosopher, and there can be nothing more impious, in the sight of heaven, than that supercilious insolence, with which, **ambitious** vanity, raised by accidental distinctions, regards those beneath it. Such a temper Jesus has forcibly reprimanded in the instance I have mentioned. " Ye call me," said Jesus, " master and lord; and ye say well, for so I am. If I, then, your lord and master, have washed your feet, ye ought also to wash one another's feet. I have given you an example, that ye should do as I have done to you." John xiii. 13, 14, 15. As if he had said, " If I, who was glorified with the father before the world was," John xvii. 5. can bend to the lowest offices; and without sullying my majesty, can perform those acts which are esteemed the most servile degradations; shall thy vanity, O man, render thee arrogant and overbearing! Shalt thou deem thyself contaminated, by any act of condescension, because thou happenest to be raised a step higher in the scale of **wealth** or **honour**, than thy brother! If I did not refuse the garb of mortality, and among mortals, the form of a servant, shalt thou, who, in the sight of heaven, art but a worm of the earth, vainly fancy thyself made of better stuff than thy fellow-worm!

That meekness of temper and gentleness of manners, which is the genuine ornament of the Christian, Jesus recommended to his disciples, in a way more persuasive and interesting, than could have been done by all the studied graces of polished eloquence. Being asked by his disciples, "Who is the greatest in the kingdom of heaven?" "he called a little child, and set him in the midst of them;"—one, who was an image of benignity and suavity of disposition; one, whose heart was not yet debased by a commerce with the world, or corroded by the passions of envy or ambition. *
"Whoever," said Jesus, "shall humble himself, as this little child, the same is greatest in the kingdom of heaven."

There is not, perhaps, a stronger indication of either

---

* See Matt. xviii.

meekness of spirit or benevolence of heart, than a kind attention to little children;—the rose-tinged symbols of unsuspicious innocence, in whose smile there is a captivation, that touches every chord of tenderness, and whose eyes, *beaming no guile*, ought to interest every beholder in their happiness. He, who can behold the smooth and benign features of infancy without emotions of complacency and fondness, hath a heart indisposed to the soft instillations of genuine benevolence. At the sight of playful childhood, our sympathy is awakened by the double attraction of it's helplessness and it's innocence; which will never fail, in the breast of the true follower of Jesus, to excite strong sensations of tenderness; which he, who does not or cannot feel, must, at least, be imbued with the venom of malignity.

Jesus seems to have considered a want of benevolence towards little children a proof of incurable depravity of heart. " Whoso," said he, " shall offend one of these little ones, it were better for him, that a millstone were hanged about his neck, and that he were drowned in the depth of the sea." Again he says; " Take heed that ye despise not one of these little ones; for I say unto you, that, in heaven, their angels do always behold the face of my father which is in heaven."*

"*Their angels do always behold the face of my father, which is in heaven.*" Who can think of this expreſſion, and dare to make the little deſtitute and *orphaned innocent* a victim of rapine, or a prey to ſorrow? Who can think of this expreſſion, when he contemplates the unwrinkled forehead of ſmiling infancy, without it's inſpiring in his breaſt the ſoft flow of thoſe benevolent ſenſations, of which language cannot convey the charm; and which, it is probable, reſemble, though in a faint degree, thoſe pleaſures which will be taſted in heaven, by " the ſpirits of good men made perfect?"

The attentive kindneſs of Jeſus, to little children, and his ſolicitude for their welfare, is no counterfeit or deceitful indication of the benevolence of his heart; of which we may gather a number of other delicate and intereſting traits, from the accounts, which the Evangeliſts have left of his amiable character.

---

* Theſe expreſſions ſeem to intimate, that little children are, in a more eſpecial manner, dear to God, and the objects of his guardian providence.

It must be remembered, that the Evangelists are no panegyrists. They are plain and artless relators of matters of fact. They make no efforts to interest the passions; they do not labour to lead men captive down the stream of their sensations. Brevity and simplicity are the characteristics of their relations; but their brevity is often more eloquent than the diffuseness of eloquence; and their simplicity, which is the earnest of their sincerity, is more interesting than the most splendid diction, elaborated into pathos, or refined into elegance.

In painting the likeness of Jesus, such as he was, and such as they knew him to be, the Evangelists do not endeavour to set off the tenderness of his nature, in the gaudy array of modern rhetoric. They delineate his feelings, by describing his acts; and they shew the kindness of his heart, by simply informing us of the extent of his beneficence.

When Simon Peter's wife's mother was dangerously ill with a fever; the Evangelist briefly tells us; " He came and *took her by the hand; and lifted her up*, and the fever left her." Mark i. 31.

When the centurion besought Jesus, for his servant who was sick of the palsy, his commiseration is not mentioned; but who does not read it in his answer? "*I will come and heal him.*"—Here, I cannot help observing, that we never hear Jesus pleading business, or the occupation of personal or temporal concerns, as an excuse for not doing good. The beneficence he exerts, he does not endeavour to magnify, as we are too apt to do, as a sacrifice of time or a neglect of other interests.

He does not vex the wretched by suspense, or by holding out hopes which were never meant to be realised. How many, among the sons of men, are solicitous to obtain, without cost, the praise of beneficence? when, perhaps, they deserve nothing but execrations, for prolonging the weariness of misery, and abusing confidence by fallacious promises, till all the energies of hope wither and perish under the anguish of disappointment. It was not so with Jesus;—he did not aggravate the sufferings of the unhappy by the bitterness of "hope deferred."

In St. Luke viii. we are told, that "a ruler of the synagogue fell down at Jesus' feet; and besought him, that he would come into his houſe; *for he had one only daughter, about twelve years of age, and ſhe lay a dying.*" It may not be amiſs to remark, what ſimplicity and yet what genuine pathos there is in this conciſe narrative.

We behold the father rent with diſtraction, at the laſt ſickneſs of an only child, throwing himſelf at the feet of Jeſus; and imploring mercy. At this affecting ſpectacle, did no tear of ſympathy ſtart into the eye of Jeſus? The Evangeliſt is ſilent;—but we learn from what follows, that Jeſus was not an unconcerned ſpectator of a father's anguiſh.

Before Jeſus could arrive at the houſe, the ruler of the ſynagogue receives a meſſage;—" Thy daughter is dead; trouble not the maſter." The ſympathiſing tenderneſs of Jeſus now ſhews itſelf; but yet it is not made, as it were, to project from the page of the hiſtorian, or to catch attention by any pomp of language or parade of ſorrow.

At the news of his daughter's death, it is probable, that the fond parent could no longer reſtrain the violence of his grief; but the divine comforter was at hand to assuage it. " Fear not," said he, " believe only and she shall be saved." This is an expression of condolence, not feigned and artificial, as the sum of human condolence usually is, but simple and sincere; kindly chasing away sorrow, and recalling the drooping eye to happiness.

When Jesus arrived at the ruler's house, he suffered none to enter, but his favourite disciples, Peter, James and John, and the father and mother of the deceased. That delicacy which characterised the benevolence of Jesus, is seen even in this little circumstance. He would not add to the affliction of the parents, by the idle gaze of thronging curiosity.

The sight of a dead corpse is, at all times, a melancholy spectacle; and more particularly so, when that corpse is *youth cut off in it's prime*. To the parents, bereft of the only pledge of their union, and hope of their age, it must have been a most excruciating and heart-rending sight. Not one, indeed, of those who were present could look on with dry eyes; " *they all wept and bewailed her.*"

Jesus, in whose breast, commiseration was never chilled by apathy, endeavours to cheer them with his accustomed simplicity of manner. "Weep not; she is not dead, but sleepeth." But "they laughed him to scorn." How natural is this part of the narrative!

In great depression of mind, when the spirits can no longer bear up against the weight that oppresses them, it is revolting to be told that our pains are imaginary, and our sorrows an illusion. "They laughed him to scorn;"—not that they would not willingly have believed his words, "she is not dead but sleepeth," true; but because they were convinced of the reality of her decease; and, perhaps, thought it a reproach on their understanding (man, even in the midst of agony, is not impervious to the touch of pride), to have an affliction imputed to fancy, which they too truly felt to be a sad reality. They, therefore, treated his suggestion with derision.

But the dead soon recovered, as if from sleep, at the energetic call of Jesus: "Maid, arise!" And he commanded to give her meat." Having restored life, his benevolence was not satisfied without annexing the means of supporting it.

Of the sympathising tenderness of Jesus, we have another very characteristic but artless relation, in Luke vii. As Jesus was approaching the city of Nain, " behold there was a dead man carried out, the only son of his mother and she was a widow." What simplicity and pathos is there in this narration! The subject is made to furnish it's own ornaments; it is cumbered with no embellishments.

The dead man, with whom the mourners were proceeding to the place of interment, " was *the only son of his mother, and she was a widow.*" After having mourned over the corpse of her husband, she was now going to behold interred in the silent grave, the only remains of their mutual affection. The son, who, perhaps, she fondly hoped would be the stay of her infirmities, and the solace of her age; and who, in the ordinary course of nature, ought to have survived her, had gone before her.

The heart of Jesus was too prone to sympathy to let

him sullenly pass by the poor destitute. "When the Lord saw her he had compassion on her;" and said unto her, with his wonted brevity, "Weep not." *He* had not learned that verbose style of condolence, which says much and means nothing. His concise "weep not," was more impressive than all the flowery tautology of modern commiseration.

"And he came and touched the bier; and they that bore him stood still;" and he exclaimed with an authority, which can either destroy the living, or animate the dead; "Young man, I say unto thee, arise! and he that was dead sat up, and began to speak." This moment stiff and motionless as a clod,—in the next, the current of life, fresh and warm, rushed into the heart; and the tongue, that was thought silent for ever, spoke again."

But the sympathising tenderness of Jesus, did not cease, while any, the least opportunity remained for it's exercise. He had raised the young man to life; but this was not enough, till he had restored him to the embraces of his mother;* and witnessed the tears of afflic-

---

* The Evangelist briefly tells us, " and he delivered him to his mother;" he does not detail the manner of doing it.

tion giving way to the warm and refreshing drops that would flow from the renewal of their mutual affection. How affecting, and yet how delicious, must this interview have been! How similar to that which departed friends will experience, when they meet again in a happier world!

We may learn, from these instances which I have adduced, and to which many others might be added, that the heart of Jesus was susceptible of the most delicate sensations of compassion;—that his benevolence was not a vapid effervescence, but fresh with life, vigorous in pursuit, unwearied in exertion, choice, not indiscriminate, in it's objects;—and that he knew how to give a softening charm to the most signal acts of beneficence, by the kindness of manner with which he performed them.

The benevolence of Jesus, though unbounded, was yet not that pretended and much-boasted sentiment of universal love, which loses sight of individual misery; and scorns the endearing ties which bind families and nations. He went about doing good; binding up the broken-hearted; pouring comfort into the bosom of the wretched. As he came to exhibit a character, proper for the imitation of man, he came adorned with all those affections, which are the brightest ornaments of our nature.

Men can never be brought to square their actions by a rule which they do not understand.—Such a rule is that of the *general good*, which Mr. Godwin recommends to his disciples, as a safe and unerring guide through the intricate maze of human intercourse; and as the best and only infallible test of justice and benevolence. By this he would appreciate the worth of the human character.

But *the general good*, is a rule of conduct which no individual can comprehend; because he can never so nicely balance the average of all the particular interests of the different parts of the community, as to know wherein the general interest resides. But though we cannot ascertain how, most effectually, to promote the general good, yet we can readily discern by what mode of conduct we can best promote the good of individuals.

Benevolence, therefore, consists in doing good to individuals, without staying nicely to examine how the good done may affect the public interest. We are not to suffer the heat of benevolence to expire, while we are making such cold-blooded calculations.

Man is the creature of sympathy; and, therefore, in his conduct to his fellow-creatures, he will be ruled by it's impulse. But no individual can sympathise with the general good, or with an impalpable abstraction; for sympathy implies distinct sensations of tenderness towards some particular object; and which, at least, in some degree, correspond with the sensations in the object by which our sympathy is excited. We can, therefore, only sympathise with the interests of individuals.

If I were to behold a person weltering in his blood or writhing in agony, from a broken limb, on the highway, he would instantly excite my sympathy; and I should endeavour to procure him relief and consolation, without once considering whether the community would be more benefited by his death than his recovery. But, according to the benevolent system of Mr. Godwin, this calculation ought to be the preliminary to any exertions of kindness; and, according to his notions, if the interests of the community could have been promoted by the death of this poor wretch, or if the relief administered could have been applied in some other way, more productive of general good, then this act of humanity would become an act of injustice.

Mr. Godwin, in his Pol. Just. b. 2. c. 2. *on justice*, intimates, that the relations of blood, of friendship and of gratitude are considerations beneath the regard of a rational being; who, in his whole conduct, ought to study the interest of the community, though at the expense of any individual, even one as dear to him as a brother, a father or a benefactor.

Mr. G. puts a case, to shew how a man ought to act, when what he calls justice clashes with sympathy.

If the palace of Fenelon, the author of Telemachus, had been on fire, and the alternative had been, that either the archbishop or his valet must perish in the flames, Mr. Godwin would have preferred preserving the life of the former, as more conducive to the general weal; even though the valet had been his brother, his father or his benefactor.

Mr. G. thinks that an individual ought to sacrifice all personal affections and duties, to that one great duty, which he owes to the community. Did man approach nearer to a state of pure intelligence, did he excel in that largeness of mind and comprehension of view, which, at one glance, could discern the aggregate interest of the body politic, his reasoning would be just; but, at present, the rule by which he proposes to regulate human conduct is much more fallible than that of sympathy, or the preference of individual good to the good of the community.

While we remain so ignorant of that in which the general weal consists, there seems no reason, why, in the vain search of an ideal good, we should exhale into airy nothingness, all the sweet though partial affections of family and of friendship. In the case which Mr. G. proposes, who would not prefer saving the life of his brother, his father or his benefactor, to that of the archbishop.

Mr. G. says, that the maxim of our Saviour, which directs us " to love our neighbour as ourselves," is not modelled with the strictness of philosophical accuracy.

It certainly does not propose, as a rule of life, a cold abstraction, intricate and embarrassing, which it must be always difficult to understand, and on which it can be seldom safe to act;—but it proposes a rule of life which comes home to every man's bosom; and of which neither the learned nor unlearned can mistake the application. It is a maxim, which he, who invariably pursues, will never act wrong. It will preserve him from every act of injustice and of inhumanity. It is a maxim, which gives life and energy to all the sweet domestic affections, which strengthens the sentiment of love, of friendship and of gratitude, and which teaches us to identify our feelings with those of wretchedness, in all it's forms.

The virtue of individuals, seems to consist not so much in serving the aggregate, as the detail of society; not so much in general as partial good; for the influence of any single act on the whole map of society, is beyond the utmost stretch of calculation.—When we behold misery in it's minute detail, we can adjust the means to the end, the relief to the necessity. It is impossible to do so, if we strive to embrace a wider sphere of action, too vast for our grasp, too immense for our discernment.

Would but individuals, with a tender and mutual benevolence, strive to promote the welfare of other individuals, dear or endeared to them, by blood, by friendship or by gratitude, or by some of the many tender incitements of sympathy, the general happiness would, ultimately, be much more effectually promoted by the beneficence of every man, directed towards particular and specific objects, than by the solitary and more ambitious exertions of each individual, to produce not partial but universal good.

I think I may safely say, that no man was ever warmed with the genuine fire of universal benevolence, while he was entirely exempt from all local and personal attachments. No good man can be insensible to the delicate and insinuating partialities of friendship, of kindred and of country. These affections are almost inseperable from our frame; and are produced by those numberless associations of ideas, and sensations of past and present time, of which we can neither calculate the power, nor controul the influence. The principle of association seems, indeed, by the wise author of all things, to have been made a part of our nature; for the purpose of connecting us by the strongest and dearest ties with our families and our homes; and making us feel, more vigorously, the inspiring glow of friendship and of patriotism.

The breast of an individual is too narrow to feel, with any distinctness, the sentiment of universal philanthropy. Our affections must, at least at first, have some distinct object on which to fix;—an object, whose magnitude is not too great for the excitement of lively and particular sensations. What is termed universal philanthropy, is merely a general and confused feeling, seldom animating to energetic action.* As we must proceed from particular to general truths, so it is from

---

* That philanthropy is counterfeit, which is not attended by benevolent sympathies and benevolent actions. Since the death of Howard, (peace to thy ashes, and glory to thy memory, thou ministering angel to the cells of misery!) Count Rumford, the poor man's patron and every man's friend, deserves the foremost rank in the list of philanthropists.— Nor can the wreath of philanthropy well be denied to the brows of Darwin and of Beddoes; whose singular ability and industry, in soothing the the most calamitous of human afflictions, and in diminishing the numerous ills, which life has to encounter from infancy to age, from the cradle to the grave, merit a statue on every shore, where the traces of humanity are to be found. Among the illustrious names, that human gratitude will transmit down the stream of time, there are few which posterity will repeat with more reverence, than those of Darwin and of Beddoes.

individual affections alone, that the soul expands to the genuine, ardent and diffusive love of the human race. From the affections of family, of friendship, and of the spot which was endeared to us by early intercourse, by tender recollection, and by numberless associations, springs the love of our country; and thence the heart kindling with increased benevolence, and catching the flame of divine love, enlarges into a wider and wider sphere, till it opens to embrace the world.

I am not, indeed, ignorant that many persons have felt the heat of the partial and local affections; have loved their kindred, their friends and their country; whose bosoms never glowed with the sentiment of universal benevolence;* and that many who have disclaimed

---

* One of the persons here alluded to, is Mr. Burke. Of the character of this extraordinary personage, I shall present the reader with a slight sketch, not drawn from personal acquaintance, but from calm reflection on his conduct and his writings.

The affections of Mr. Burke all gravitated towards his kindred, incapable of a wider expansion. Of philanthropy, he possessed but little; or he would not have struggled so long, and with so much energy and obstinacy, to produce the extermination, by fire and sword, of twenty-four million of his fellow-men. His morality was neither enlarged by a diffusive benevolence, nor animated by an enlightened piety. His friendship was warm while it lasted; but it was liable to be interrupted by the irri-

the tender charities of family, friends and kindred, have loudly boasted of being fired with the spirit of universal

---

table petulance of his temper. Inflated with the pride of genius, he was impatient of contradiction; and his resentments were, in more than one instance, indulged even to bitterness.

His fame, with posterity, will rest chiefly on the splendour of his eloquence; but this being employed rather in the embellishment of prejudices that are evanescent, than in support of principles that are immortal; I doubt whether it have earned him a wreath of glory, that may wave defiance to the rage of time. His style, as an orator, is vehement, impetuous, and often highly impassioned; fraught with the beautiful combinations of genius, and displaying the magnificent decorations of an exuberant fancy; but he is rarely discriminated by those sublime conceptions, which arise from comprehensive views, and which mark an intellect of the highest order. His wit sparkles with brilliancy; it's flashes often captivate as much by their justness as their splendour; but he sometimes pursues them till they lose their lustre, and languor takes place of astonishment.

When he attempts to reason in a logical order, his arguments, too often, resemble the Sibyl's leaves; they are dispersed in a moment, by the breath of his imagination. His judgment may, for a while, rule his fancy; but his fancy always, at last, succeeds in ruling his judgment.

He was well acquainted with men, and with human affairs in their little detail; but he does not seem to have considered, like a philosopher, the general principles, or like a benevolent Christian, the general interests of human nature. His political reasonings are often weak, because they are taken entirely from partial views, and from fleeting interests; and do not rest on the basis of eternal and unchangeable truth. Could he have effected his wishes, he would have established an oligarchy of wealth and rank, on the ruins of the rights of mankind. He would have placed the liberties of the people on no firmer basis than that of the concessions of the crown; and he would have despoiled the monarchy of those wholesome

Philanthropy.* With respect to those of the first class, I strongly suspect that it will be found, that their affec-

---

limitations, which are a source of happiness both to the prince and to the people.

The principles of Mr. Burke, seem to have been rather modified by his interest, than his interest by his principles. His principal pursuit was private emolument; but he endeavoured to impress on others, till perhaps he had impressed on himself, the conviction that it was the public good. His private embarrassments, increased by inattention and profuseness, unfortunately for his country and for the world, rendered him venal; and, if we may judge from his sentiments on the resistance of America, his opinions on the French revolution, were less swayed by his conscience than his pension.——Possessing those energies of genius, which, taking an independent direction, might have rendered him as much the benefactor as he was the ornament of his species; his talents contributed but little to enlarge the stock of wisdom; and though they have rendered some service to taste, and have diversified the elegant combinations of language; yet these are but paltry benefits, compared with the miseries of that desolating contest, in which, they contributed to involve his country.

* Rousseau has been too often extolled as a philanthropist. Mr. Burke said of him, that he loved his kind and hated his kindred.—The exposure of his children, by whatever sophistry it may be excused, is an indelible blot on his humanity; and invalidates all his pretensions to philanthropy. For, can that philanthropy be genuine, which is founded on the extinction of the parental affections; and which, with more than savage brutality, forsakes the poor innocents, it brings into the world?

Every page of Rousseau glows with the captivations of that sentimental luxury, of which he is so great a master; and which he arrays in all the blandishments of eloquence. Hence the source of that admiration, which his writings have so universally excited. Though his judgment, as a philosopher, was not so profound; yet his taste was so exquisite, that

tions were prevented, by narrow prejudices, from a wider expansion. Of the last class, I fear that the

---

he strews flowers in the most rugged way, and interests the passions and the fancy, in the investigation of the most abstract propositions. This is his great excellence.

In his new Eloise, the interest consists, not so much in the diversity or the combination of the incidents, as in the beauty of the sentiment and the magic of the diction. The picture of Julia, is highly finished; but it leaves on the mind more impressions of respect, than of tenderness, of admiration than of love.—At times, she appears an heterogeneous mixture of apathies and passion, of prudence and of coquetry. In some situations she wants tenderness; in others firmness; and she is often less governed by the warm impulses of affection, than by the abstractions of philosophy.

His Emilus, though marked by the illuminating touches and the original conceptions of genius, yet, considered as a system, is more conspicuous for it's singularity than it's truth. It pourtrays a system of education, which, if it were universally adopted, would keep the human species in a state of permanency between light and darkness, between savage barbarity and civilized refinement. It would counteract the moral and physical improvement of man; the progress of knowledge and the productiveness of industry.

Though Rousseau had little beneficence, yet his writings, breathing nothing but the reciprocal love and kindness and confidence of the Golden Age, contributed, by their wide diffusion and their enchanting eloquence to render humanity fashionable; and they have, at least, this merit, —that no man can well rise from reading them, without feeling a higher respect for his species.

That extreme and febrile sensibility, which was the characteristic peculiarity of Rousseau, while it proved the origin of many of his miseries, was, perhaps, a principal source of his greatness. It imparted a singular delicacy, freshness and animation to every page of his writings.—His

majority are usually men of little virtue and less sensibility; too cold for friendship; too inert for beneficence; and claiming the wreath of philanthropy, without deserving it by any acts of humanity.

---

feelings, in whatever channel they flowed, rushed on with a resistless impetuosity; but, in the end, they made a wreck of his understanding. His judgment was lost in the unremitting turbulence of his sensations; and in some intervals of insanity, he exhibited the melancholy prospect of genius crumbling into ruins.

The language of Rousseau, was always a faithful mirror of what was passing in the heart; which now thrilled with rapture, and now raged with passion. Of his style, the peculiar characteristic, is exuberance of imagery; profusion, without distinction of lustre. It often resembles a landscape, in which there is a great assemblage of beautiful forms, without any intermediate spots of barrenness; but without any objects of a striking and prominent grandeur; and, in the contemplation of which, the eye is, at last, satiated by the uniformity.—Yet, highly coloured as is the eloquence, of Rousseau, I believe that the generality of readers would peruse his works with less relish, if they were less adorned. And, it must be confessed, that the ornaments with which they are embellished, are not the frippery and patchwork of a paltry artist, but the rich copiousness of an highly saturated imagination; and they often possess a charm, of which, even the apathy of the coldest critic can hardly be insensible to the fascination.—He who wishes to perfect himself in those delicacies of language or curious felicities of phraseology, which impress a palpable form, a living entity on the fleeting tints and sensations of the heart, should carefully analyse the genius of the style of Rousseau; should search into the causes, from which result the beauty and splendour of his combinations; and endeavour to extract, from an attentive perusal of the Eloise and the Emilius, a portion of that taste by which they were inspired.

Individuals ourselves, our affections (if I may use a quaint expression) have a natural tendency towards individuality. He who pretends to love all persons alike, really loves none. There can, in the human breast, be no general and universal, without some partial affections. It is from the combination of particular sympathies, of personal and local attachments, that we at last imbibe the flame of a comprehensive and boundless benevolence.

The breast of Jesus was certainly warmed with the brightest fires of universal love; but that love did not extinguish the lesser charities. The spirit of philanthropy did not liberate him from the tender bondage of local and personal attachments. His heart was not insensible to the sympathies of private friendship.* Tho' he selected twelve persons to be his disciples and constant companions; yet of these twelve he seems to have regarded three, Peter, James, and John, † with a more

---

* See John xi. 5.

† They alone of his disciples were permitted to be present at his transfiguration, and during his agony in the garden. See Matt. xxvi. 37. The Evangelists have exhibited the character of Peter, more distinctly than

peculiar and affectionate confidence; and of these three, one is emphatically styled " the Apostle whom Jesus

---

that of the other apostles.—The passions of Peter were strong, but they were not under the controul of his discretion. His attachment to his master, partaking of his constitutional vivacity, was fervent and sincere; but, like most men of a sanguinary temperament, he seems to have been governed rather by impulse than reflection. The impetuosity of his temper often embarrassed him in errors; and his first emotions were too vehement to be lasting.—What he felt, he felt strongly; but the violence of his sensations occasioned him to over-look the disproportion between his strength and his resolutions. From the effervescence of heroism, he sunk into the languor of cowardice.—He had zeal—but it was not moderated by prudence, nor confirmed by perseverance. He was ready to encounter danger, without measuring it's magnitude; eager in pursuit, he looked only at the end, without regarding it's intermediate obstacles. One instant we behold him plunging into the sea, impatient to meet Jesus, and made buoyant by faith, walking steadily on the waters—the next, he faulters on the billows, and exclaims, in despondency, " **Lord, help** me, **I perish!**"—When his master was apprehended, he **instantly drew his** sword; and, in a moment of passion, prepared, **like a brave** man, for resistance; but when he saw the soldiers leading Jesus away to judgment, he followed the pusillanimous example of the apostles, who " forsook him and fled."—Still the emotions of fear seems to have been soon replaced by that of affection; and Peter was never backward in obeying the impulse of his sensations. He got admission into the hall of judgment; and, here, we might suppose that he **would not have** appeared, unless **he** had summoned courage to avow himself, **and to live or** to perish with **his master.**—But far otherwise; his fortitude is no sooner put to the test, than he even denies all knowledge of Jesus; and, like most persons who are conscious of falshood, he endeavours to strengthen the weakness of his assertions, by the effrontery of oaths and the wickedness of perjuries.—But observe the

loved."* John was the congenial friend of his soul; and dear to him, as Jonathan was to David.

Striped of the sweet domestic affections, and destitute of the love of friends or kindred, how naked, desolate and cheerless would the heart of man be!!! Where, in misery, should we seek for refuge or for sympathy, if the benevolent system of some late moralists were to be permitted to freeze into a cold, insensate mass every warm drop of happiness which is instilled into the heart, by the tender connections of family and of friendship?

No man can live long in the world, without contracting some individual attachments. A congeniality of sentiments, or of manners, among those with whom we mingle in the intercourse of life, will, naturally,

---

rapid vicissitude of his sensations! *One look* from his suffering master, whom he had so lately and so resolutely denied, was sufficient to melt him into tears and to rend him with remorse.—" He went out, and wept bitterly."—Such was Peter! and such, alas! is too often the chequered image of those, who are most renowned for their virtue or their piety!

* The character of John, which rendered him worthy of being beloved by Jesus, seems to have been distinguished by the most amiable benevolence. His Epistles inculcate love to mankind, as the sum of all religion. See 1 John iii. 11, 14, 17, 18, 23; and iv. 7, 8, 11, 12, 16, 20, 21.

excite a stronger degree of affection towards them, than towards others. Though friendship may subsist, and perhaps with great liveliness of sensations, where there are some few dissimilitudes of temper, of genius and manners, yet it cannot be cemented among those, between whom there is, in those respects, a total and irreconcileable discordancy.—Friendship derives it's energy and it's spirit from the power of sympathy. We naturally love those most, in whose company we enjoy the greatest degree of pleasurable sensation; and this we certainly must do, with those whose habits approach the nearest to our own; with whom we can indulge a bland communion of happiness, to whom we can impart our joys and sorrows, sure of their exciting corresponding vibrations in their sympathetic bosoms.

It is observable, that those of the same family are usually most attached to each other, who are most associated in the intercourse of childhood. Constant intercourse tends to wear away the asperities and dissimilitudes of disposition, in which they differ from each other, as individuals; and to bring them, in some measure to a common likeness. It strengthens the affections of kindred, by the more powerful influence of sympathy,

Brothers and sisters, who see little of each other, and, in whom, the ties of nature are not invigorated by a constant and endearing intercourse, and, particularly, at that period when the heart is most sensative to tender impressions, most ready to assimilitate itself to the dispositions of those around it, and to cast, as it were, anew, in the mould of association, have seldom any more than a very slight regard for each other;—a regard that may be just kept alive by a sense of duty; but which glows not with the fondness of love. Affection arises from frequently placing ourselves in the situations of others, from being allotted a share in their joys and sorrows, from a kind interchange of sentiments and interests, from the impalpable agency of a thousand nameless sympathetic attractions, and is therefore chilled and withered without continual intercourse.

Friendship, when it is warm, genuine and sincere, partakes in a great measure of the sacredness of the kindred affections. It supposes an identity of interests, a communion of sensations, a reciprocity of love. Our friend is to us as a brother.

Jesus well knew that a tender and reciprocal friendship can gladden the melancholy path of human life. He therefore sanctioned, by his example, that pure flame of private friendship, which inspires different persons with an identity of interests, and which, while it increases the happiness of individuals, need substract nothing from the sum of general benevolence.

That Jesus was neither an enemy nor a stranger to the tender sympathies, we may learn from various parts of the Evangelic memoirs; and, particularly, from his behaviour on the occasion of Lazarus's death, which is related in John xi. and which places the messenger of immortality in a light equally amiable and interesting.

The Evangelist tells us, in his plain and artless way, that " Jesus loved Martha, and her sister, and Lazarus." Lazarus being taken ill, his sisters sent Jesus this concise but affecting message. " Lord, *he whom thou lovest* is sick." More, certainly, was not wanting to work on our Saviour's tenderness. Of course, we might expect to read, that he hastened, without delay, to the sick bed of his friend.—No; he waited two days in the place where he was.—But was it apathy? was it insensibility to the call of suffering friendship?—No; the delay was certainly as painful to Jesus as it was to the sisters of Lazarus.—But Providence never sends his sunshine but in the fullest seasons; and Jesus manifested the wisdom as well as the goodness of his father, who often sees it best, for awhile, to withhold his blessings, even from those he loves.

In the mean time Lazarus died. Had Jesus been present, he knew that he could not have resisted the languishing looks of his friend, or the solicitations of his sisters, to save him ere he died.—He therefore prudently declined going to the house till after his death. This is plainly intimated in the speech, of Jesus to his disciples. "I am glad," said he, "for your sakes, that I was not there to the intent that ye may believe; nevertheless let us go unto him."

Martha, as soon as she heard that Jesus was coming, went and met him; but Mary sat still.—By the by, how well does this little incident mark the characteristic eagerness of Martha, and the graver and more pensive turn of Mary? and how well does it agree with what St. Luke x. has related of the two sisters; of whom Martha is said to be "cumbered about much serving,"

while Mary " sat at Jesus' feet, and heard his word?"
—How well is the unity of characters supported in the four Evangelists, and what can better prove that they are not the historians of fiction but of facts; and that they had seen and conversed with the persons they describe?—To pass from this digression: " Lord, if thou hadst been here," said Martha, to Jesus, with her natural impatience, " My brother had not died!"—" Thy brother," said Jesus, " shall rise again;" and again he gives the same assurance, with more than usual energy and solemnity. " I am the resurrection and the life; he that believeth in me, though he were dead, yet shall he live; and whosoever liveth and believeth in me shall never die."—Martha now left Jesus to call her sister Mary, who, " when she had come where Jesus was, and saw him, fell down at his feet; saying unto him, Lord, if thou hadst been here, my brother had not died!"—When Jesus beheld Mary, her sister, and their friends overwhelmed in misery, he seems to have been deeply affected. The Evangelist describes his grief in these plain but strong terms. " He groaned in the spirit and was troubled;" and again " Jesus wept!" Overcome by the tenderness of his nature, he could not restrain the sigh of sympathy or the tear of friendship. The

violence of his sorrow seems to have excited the notice of the Jews; who, either from the sudden impulse of admiration, or of envy, exclaimed: " Behold, *how* he loved him!"—Jesus now, " groaning in the spirit," goes up to the tomb, in which his friend was laid, and exclaims, in a voice which, at the last hour, will awaken the myriads of myriads that have passed into the regions of forgetfulness, " Lazarus, come forth." In an instant, the spirit of life returned to the body, which had begun to pass into corruption.

The behaviour of Jesus, in this scene of affliction, speaks, in the most captivating manner, the tenderness of his feelings, and the warmth of his affections.—His friendship was not a sickly and transitory glow of fondness, the mere vapour of caprice, or the ebullition of appetite;—it did not originate from a familiarity in vice, nor was it polluted by the base alloy of venality and interest.—It was a friendship excited by sympathy, cherished by benevolence and preserved by esteem.—It was formed of elements, not perishable, but immortal; —a friendship, which death does not extinguish; but only transfers it into some happier country; and places it in circumstances more genial to it's growth, and more auspicious to it's expansion; where no storms can shake the firmness of it's roots, and no blights wither the beauty of it's branches.

As Jesus was not insensible to friendship, neither was he callous to the affections, which ought to unite kindred blood.—When agonizing on the cross, his own pains did not make him forgetful of his mortal mother. He saw her standing by his cross; the thought of her destitute condition awakened his sympathy; and he commended her, with peculiar earnestness, to the care of his beloved disciple. "Behold," said he to the Evangelist, "thy mother!" The most elaborate recommendation could not have said more; and more was not necessary to be said, to make the Apostle feel the love of a son for the mother of his dying master.

Providence, by having distributed mankind into families, and willed the relations of husband and wife, father and child, of brother and sister, hath impressed the seal of sacredness on the kindred affections. But though nature has sown the seeds of these affections, yet they will not shoot up and blossom without careful cultivation. They require the benign and fostering breath of sympathy, to bring them to a vigorous maturity, and to enable them to stand against the changes and inclemencies of life. But the kindred affections, when they have been strengthened by a long and continued interchange of kindnesses, and by a multiplicity of agreeable associations, are a source of pure and exquisite happiness. They resemble that fragrant incense of piety, which the Spirit of love wafts from the heart of the righteous to the throne of the Eternal.

Of all the affections which can warm the heart of man, that of conjugal love, which unites the blandishments of all the kindred charities, with a thousand additional captivations, seems the best adapted to increase the sum of human happiness. Perhaps, on no occasion, did Jesus more clearly demonstrate his knowledge of the genuine source of social and domestic bliss, than in the restraints which he imposed on the nuptial union. He did not consider marriage as a mere transient association, to be formed as the appetite prompts, and to be dissolved as it decays.

Our Saviour evidently considers marriage as a religious obligation. He says, Matt. x. xi. 6. "What

God hath joined together, let no man put asunder." He here consecrates the relations of man and wife, by the sanctions of the divine law; which is superior in force to any civil institutions.—Civil institutions may prescribe the outward form, according to which, marriage shall be celebrated; but the outward form, by no means, constitutes the sacredness of marriage in a religious view. The outward form gives the sanction of decency to the union of the sexes; but that union, will still partake of the essence of prostitution, unless it be associated with the inward sense of a divine obligation, feelingly impressed on the conscience of the contracting parties. Wherever matrimony is entered into without any religious considerations of the moral duties it enjoins, it is a sensual, profane and unhallowed connexion.

Regarding marriage on Christian principle, nothing but actual adultery can justify it's dissolution; and, in all cases, adultery, wherever it is clearly established, ought, instantly, to cancel the validity of the marriage. —Nay, in the eye of the Almighty, one adulterous desire, breathing it's pollution on the heart, stains it with the guilt of adultery. Matt. v. 28.

Were we to regard marriage, without any relation to the divine law or to the Christian sanctions, as a mere civil contract, then there would, no longer, be any reason, why it should not cease when it became mutually disagreeable to the parties concerned; when it disappointed their mutual expectations, and they ceased to will it's continuance. In this case, a mere incompatibility of temper, would be a sufficient ground for a divorce. But to allow this, would be to offer a premium upon the universality of prostitution; and to make the nuptials of mankind as transient as those of brutes.

The disposition of individuals is as various as their features. No two tempers can be precisely similar; and a difference in this respect, is no better argument for a divorce, than a difference of complexion. The tender associations of familiar intercourse, where marriage is entered into, with a sense of it's religious obligations, soon wear away the discrepancies of the most discordant tempers; and smooth off the harsh incongruities of taste and manners. Both parties will consent to forego their mutual asperities, by a mutual accommodation.

Whether we regard it in it's political importance, or it's subserviency to social and individual bliss, the marriage-tie cannot be confidered as too facred. It is marriage which renovates the world. It is the trunk, from which germinate all the domeftic charities, that bear the fruits of happinefs.

Thofe who would diveft matrimony of it's religious fanctions, would ftrip it of all it's moral, and even wither the bloom of it's phyfical attractions. It would foon fink into a debafed and brutal connection; a fordid league for avarice or for luft.

It is not the mere name or ceremony of marriage, that renders it facred. Every marriage, which is not contracted from a fenfe of mutual efteem, which is not fublimed by the endearments of fympathy, and hallowed by the fpirit of piety, is vitally and effentially proftitution. The only true and genuine marriage, is that which is an union of mind and foul, as well as appetite; not fpringing from the inconfiderate tumult of paffion, but the confiderate tranquillity of efteem; not volatile, but permanent; not exhaled from humour and whim, but combined with all the beft affections of the heart; and faftened on the confcience, by the glorifying energies of religion.

In the brutes, there is nothing which can deserve the the name of conjugal affection. Their union terminates with the impulse of the moment. In man it is far otherwise.—In man, conjugal love assumes a moral complexion. A thousand associations, blend it with a thousand captivations. It is refined by sympathy; it is sublimed by fancy; till, losing half it's animal grossness it resembles the delicate intercourse of purer spirits.

In man, the imagination, inspired by the passion of love, adorns the beloved object with numberless attractions; and forms a picture of perfection incompatible with the frailties of humanity.—But the time, at last, comes when the first warm transports of sensibility yield to the calmer emotions; the conjugal tie, familiarised, breaks the spell of the enchantress.

Then, when experience shades with traces of frailty the blameless picture which fancy drew,—then happy is it, if, when the first blaze of transport is over, it leave behind it, that bland warmth of mutual esteem, which leads through life, at that medium of temperature, which is equally distant from rapturous fondness, and from negligent indifference.

The ravished inquietudes of sensation, and the extacies of imagination are too violent to be lasting; but that mutual esteem which is spiritualised by the breath of religion, will survive the gay illusions of fancy; and, instead of being abated, will be increased, as time nips the bloom of youth, and the heart grows chill with the touch of age.—Nay, it is probable that the pure and genuine flame of affection, which identified the interests and the sensations of two hearts, on this earth, will shine for ever in a better country. Death will not dissolve the true undissembled union of souls.—Hence, then, take comfort, thou wretched mourner, who art following to the grave one, who was long the fond companion of thy travel in the waste of misery!

Our Saviour said, that, in heaven, they neither marry nor are given in marriage; but are like the angels. The physical bonds of love will perish in the grave; but it's moral bonds—the delicate energies of sympathy—will be everlasting.

As there are some affections which attach us to individuals, so there are others which connect us, by bonds of tenderness, with the great mass of society. As we are sensible to the glow of filial, parental, conjugal and friendly love, so we ought to be alive to the patriotic affections, which incline our hearts to sympathise with the welfare of the community, to which we belong, and the country, in which we were born.

Some have, indeed, thought that the heat of patriotism, which a good man feels for the welfare of his native country, ought to be extinguished in the spirit of more comprehensive patriotism, which attaches him to the universal welfare of his species; without any partial or peculiar concern for the people, among whom he was bred, or the country, in which he was born.

But, I think, that no man, unless he have wandered, from his very infancy, like a vagabond, over the earth, without ever tasting or communicating the comforts of domestic society, can well overcome those early associations, which endear him to the fields of his youth; and which, as it were, assimilate his nature to the language, to the manners, and the interests of his native country. For that country can he refrain from burning with some sparks of a peculiar fondness? Is such a partiality criminal? Is it not rather a virtue, which association produces, but which heaven approves? For, among every people, of every clime, whether barbarous or civilised, whether inhabiting spots of luxuriant fertility, or of eternal barrenness, the love of the " natale solum" has ever been a predominant passion: of which the extinction would cover the various regions of the earth with shades of melancholy, and dry up the perennial source of their interest, their captivations and their charms.* That philosophy, therefore, appears to me

---

* The power of association, over the affections, will be seen in the instance which I am going to mention, from Captain Cooke's last voyage to the Pacific Ocean. On Captain Clerke's arrival at the town of St. Peter and St. Paul, in Kamschatka, Mr. King, Mr. Webster and others were dispatched to the commanding officer, at Belcheretsk; on their way, they were hospitably entertained, at the little village of Karatchin. Whilst they were dining, in a miserable hut, the guests of absolute strangers, and at the extremity of the habitable globe, a solitary half-worn pewter spoon soon attracted their attention. " It's form," says the narrator, " was familiar to us; and the word London was stamped upon the back of it. It is impossible to express the anxious hopes and tender remembrances this excited in us. Those, who have been long absent from their native country, will readily conceive what inexpressible pleasure such trifling incidents can give."

On the subject of association, I shall dwell a little longer. Most of our pleasures are derived from this source. In the views of nature, many prospects excite agreeable sensations, which have nothing beautiful in themselves; and, for which, no other cause can be assigned, than that these prospects bear a resemblance to those which were connected by us, in our infancy, with agreeable sensations. These sensations were excited by causes

of a pernicious cast, which would reduce the affections to an uniform level; which would make an Englishman, as zealous for the prosperity of France, or of China, or

---

foreign to the beauty of the view itself; but which, in the lapse of time, have been intimately blended with it, and become parts of it. Similar views then produce the very sensations, which originated from associated ideas. The sight of fields, which, in their form and position, resemble those in which our early days were spent, would inspire us with delightful emotions; and, at first, without our knowing why; for, we should not immediately recollect the similitude. Ideas of pleasure, having been associated with particular forms, or with this or that disposition of country, are subject to frequent revival, when the causes which first produced them are forgotten.—We generally attach the idea of beauty to smooth undulating surfaces; and the contemplation of them, arises, in the heart, feelings that please. The first pleasures of men are excited by their mothers breast,—the agreeable sensations which the infant experiences in sucking, are, afterwards, attached to the softness, smoothness and whiteness of the milky fountain. His eyes feast on it with placid rapture; his little fingers move, in various directions, gently, over the swelling breast. Surfaces that have similar spiral and waving lines, afterwards excite similar emotions.—There is, perhaps, nothing either beautiful or ugly, but as it is associated with ideas of pleasure or aversion, or with circumstances which have, some way or other, interested our feelings, or influenced our enjoyments.

A good-natured German, in a journey, which he made on foot, thro' several parts of England, says—" When I was past Bakewell, a place far inferior to Derby, I came by the side of a broad river, to a small eminence, where a fine cultivated field lay before me. This field, all at once, made an indescribable and very pleasing impression on me; *which, at first, I could not account for; till I recollected having seen, in my childhood, near the village where I was educated, a situation strikingly similar to that now before me in England.* See Travels by C. P. Moritz. 12mo. Robinsons.—See likewise Zoonom. vol. i. 145.

Siberia, as for that of Britain; and extinguish the partial flame of all local sympathies.

Patriotism, like extension, must begin at a point; but may be increased, by gradual diffusion, till it becomes a philanthropy, that knows no limits than the limits of nature. But as the circulation near the heart is more warm, fresh and vigorous than at the extremities, so, every man's affection for his native country ought to be more fervent and vivid, than that philanthropic heat which may interest him in the happiness of distant regions.

A good Christian will be a citizen of his own country, before he will claim the too often affected appellation of a citizen of the world; a name frequently abused to disguise a base insensibility to the best affections of the human heart.

But, though a good Christian will glory in a partial fondness for his own country, still he will feel a lively interest for the happiness of other nations. He will love justice and benevolence even more than his country; and he will never consent to violate these sacred principles, though, by the violation, he might increase her oppulence or her grandeur.

It is a very common notion, that kingdoms sink in misfortunes, in proportion, as their neighbours rise in prosperity.—Hence, that mean jealousy and rivalry, that separates and imbitters the great brotherhood of mankind. Hence, so much bloodshed, and so many wars.—Nations do not consider that they ought rather to rejoice at, than to lament the increase of each other's wealth and happiness.

Prosperity is not confined to one single channel; it has numerous channels, which communicate with and assist each other. The prosperity of our neighbours always tends, sooner or later, to augment our own.

The want of that benevolence, which is of the true Christian sort, prevents states as well as individuals from discerning their real and essential interest. Most nations thirst, with the greediness of monopolists, for an exclusive commerce; of which they may prevent their neighbours from any participation of the advantages. But this is a delusive policy, which promises great and produces little benefit. *For, it is for the good of mankind, that prosperity should run in many channels; as the power of it's production is always increased, in proportion to the multiplication of it's sources.*

Nations, at present, boast most loudly of turning the balance of trade against each other; but, I trust that the time is approaching, when the rivalry of avarice shall be extinguished; and kingdoms shall look for glory only in the rivalry of benevolence.

To enrich his native country, a good Christian will never be an advocate for oppressing a weaker neighbour; he will scorn to carry fire and sword, devastation and murder into a foreign kingdom, to promote the fancied glory or security of his own. A good Christian will consider war as murder, with an infinite aggravation of it's atrocity; and he will refuse to unsheath the sword, except in the single case of the aggressions of tyranny, either from without or from within; and then he will cheerfully hazard his fortune, and shed his blood in the defence of his country, and for the preservation of her liberties and her laws.

Such will be a good political Christian; such we may

without any impiety, imagine that Jesus would have been,* were he living on earth, as a man, in the society

---

* Some divines have endeavoured to persuade us, that the Author of Christianity was an advocate for passive political servitude.—In the whole compass of the Evangelic memoirs, I know but one passage, which has any direct relation to the important topic of civil obedience.—The Jews having asked Jesus, whether it were lawful to give tribute unto Cæsar or not. He replied, "Why tempt ye me, ye hypocrites? Shew me the tribute money. And they brought unto him a penny. And he faith unto them, Whose is this image and superscription? They say unto him, Cæsar's; then faith he unto them, *Render therefore unto Cæsar, the things that are Cæsar's; and unto God, the things that are God's.*" In the first place; "Render unto Cæsar, &c." means, give to Cæsar *his just dues*; but then this point remains to be considered. *What are the just dues of Cæsar?* And this question is not to be determined by the arbitrary will of Cæsar, **but by the** considerations of religion, of justice and humanity. Were we to permit Cæsar to determine his own rights and prerogative, according to his own caprice, we give him a licence to trample on the sacred rights of conscience and of justice. This was not the intention of Jesus; for he **has qualified the** obedience commanded **on the** first **part of** the sentence, "**Render, &c.**" by the restriction which is employed in the last,—"*but* unto God the things that are God's."

A good Christian will cheerfully pay tribute, to whom tribute is due, custom to whom custom, honour to whom honour; but if obedience be demanded of him, in cases where he cannot conscientiously pay it, he will courageously resist the tyranny that demands it. He will "not fear him who can kill the body, but him who can destroy both body and soul in hell."

Man was not made by heaven for a slave. This truth is written, by the hand of God, on every man's heart; and it is a palpable and self-evident proposition to every one, whose mind has not been totally imbruted by long continued habits of obsequiousness to the scourge of slavery, and the lash of oppression.

of men. In his character, we meet with several traits of that national attachment which is the essence of patriotism. In Luke xix. we read, that Jesus, descending from the Mount of Olives, wept when he beheld the city, and the temple which was the boast of every Jew, and the glory of his native land; but which he knew would, in a few years, present only a melancholy scene of ruin and devastation. This thought roused an exclamation of patriotic sympathy. "Would thou had known," said he, "even thou, at least in this thy day, the things which belong unto thy peace!—But now they are hid from thine eyes!" The storm of divine fury, which was gathering against his country, he saw; and he struggled in vain to avert, by reformation and repentance. His countrymen were blind to the danger, and insensible to his exhortations. But Jesus, unable to bring the Jews to a serious sense of the calamities, which were impending over them, and to open their eyes to the light of the gospel of immortality, instead of execrating, with bitterness, lamented with tenderness their blindness and depravity. "O Jerusalem," said he, "O Jerusalem, thou that killest the prophets, and stonest them which are sent unto thee, how often would I have gathered thy children together, even as a hen gathereth her chickens under her wings, and ye would not!" Matt. xxiii. With artlefs but impaffioned eloquence, he mourned over the wilful obftinacy of his beloved city. He difcovers the fervency of a patriot, whofe affections centre in the welfare of his country; and whofe foul breathes the warmeft wifhes for it's profperity.

A good Chriftian will be a ftrenuous defender of public virtue and public piety. He will regard the decay of morality and of religion, as the greateft calamity that can befal his country; and as the fure indication of a declining empire. He, who, in a public ftation, can countenance the leaft relaxation of public integrity, or abet the abafement of the national character, by any acts of injuftice or of inhumanity, by the violation of any one focial or facred tie, is no Chriftian, but an enemy to Chriftianity. A good Chriftian will glow with an honeft zeal, to preferve the religion which he venerates from any contaminating mixture—from hypocrify and from bigotry—from that foppery of worfhip, which mocks the Supreme Intelligence—and from that extravagance and enthufiafm, which conceals the light of heaven under clouds and darknefs.

Christianity has been frequently, though I trust undesignedly, injured by those who are sometimes falsely stiled Evangelical preachers; who, losing sight of the rational practice of the gospel, talk of nothing but what they call it's doctrines; but of which, it is plain, that as they know nothing themselves, they cannot make them clear to others. By pretending to explain those things, of which they have no distinct and definite ideas, they are betrayed into the grossest inconsistencies, and often the most ludicrous absurdities. The sublime morality which Jesus inculcated, and which impresses the spirit of charity by the most awful sanctions, they pass over in contemptuous silence; while they vainly labour to *unfold the dark covering of the ark* of the Christian mysteries. *

---

* The turn of these expressions is borrowed from a Mss. of Chatterton, in which he makes the fictitious Rowley offer to refute " at St. Mark's cross, in the church-yard of St. Mary Redcleff," in Bristol, the heretical notions of John a Milverton, who seems to have embraced the doctrines of Socinus. The passage I allude to, is as follows: " It is in vain for the wit of man, to pretend to unfold the dark covering of the ark of the Trinity; least, like those of old, he be stricken dead and his reason lost, by breathing in an element too fine and subtle for his gross nature."

I shall here say something on the subject of the Pseudo-Rowley,—a subject to which I have given much attention; as is well known to my

As the pretended Evangelical preachers affect to preach nothing but Jesus, it is strange that they should so

---

friends; and particularly my much esteemed friend, Charles Gower, M. D. of Oriel College; a gentleman, distinguished by the integrity of his conduct, the openness and kindness of his heart, and the diversified copiousness of his erudition.

Thomas Chatterton, one of the most extraordinary personages that has appeared in the present century, was born at Bristol, Nov. 20, 1752. His prediliction for antiquities was excited in his childhood. He seems, likewise, when almost an infant, to have imbibed a passion for fame, and a thirst for distinction. Traces of this were visible in his earliest intercourse.

He always ambitiously sought the post of pre-eminence among his play-fellows. He was not willing to consider them as his equals; he would have them his servants. How often might the dawn of character be observed in the sports and amusements of youth?

In the mind of young Chatterton, the love of pre-eminence was an impetuous and ruling passion. It imparted an unwearied activity to the energies of his mind; and inspired him with vigor, to resist that lassitude which arises from incessant exertion. In his meals, he used an almost ascetic abstinence; and he slept but little. The greater part of every night he devoted to the multiform occupations of genius; his unquenchable passion for fame almost enabled him to counteract the ordinary calls of nature for repose; and without a considerable portion of which common mortals would soon expire.

To the early thirst of Chatterton for distinction, and which, more fortunately for the world than for himself, took a literary direction, I attribute his forgery of the poems attributed to Rowley. He well knew that any poems, appearing in his own name, and as the productions of a parish-boy, would have excited but little attention; and he certainly could not hope that they would cause his reputation to emerge from the bosom of obscurity. But he knew that the publication of poems, said to

rarely recommend to the imitation and the practice of of their followers, the striking lineaments of his charac-

have been written in the fifteenth century, and with all the harmony of numbers, which is perceptible in the writers of the eighteenth, would be a literary phenomenon, well calculated to excite general curiosity. Even in Bristol, where the heart is too usually dormant to any emotions, but to those of gain or of voluptuousness, a few sparks of curiosity and of interest were elicited; and Chatterton found the shadow of patronage (alas, it was but the shadow!) in a surgeon and a pewterer.

Another motive, which operated to the production of this wonderful **forgery, was** the desire of the young author to gratify his vanity, by impo**sing on the learned** world. This he did most effectually. The garb of antiquity, which he assumed, seems to have deceived some of the most profound antiquaries; and the genuineness of the poems, might, to this **day,** have remained a matter of ambiguity, if the forgery of Chatterton had not been indisputably established by the taste of Wharton, and the precise and penetrating erudition of **Tyrwhit.**

The most remarkable circumstance, **in the life of Chatterton, is the** early maturity **of his mind.** His intellect, un**like the intellect** of most men, does not **seem to have attained** it's greatness by a slow and gradual, but a **rapid and almost instantaneous** expansion.———Of that taste, whose **divine irradiations are dispensed to none** but the man of genius,—of that taste, **which is a** subtle and delicate emanation from a sound judgment, quick perceptions and a vigorous intelligence, and which bestows the **power of** discerning beauties that are invisible to vulgar apprehensions, **and of** forming combinations which strike universally by their justness or dazzle by their splendour,—Chatterton possessed a more than common share, at a premature period.

At the age of sixteen, he produced the tragedy of Ælla; in which there are the marks **of a** mind vigorous in pursuit, powerful in combination and delicate in selection.— In the perusal of Ælla, who, that can sympathise with the varied agitations of the human breast, can refrain from expe-

ter, and the most prominent features of his doctrine! In a cant unmeaning jargon, they talk much of vital

---

riencing alternate emotions of softness and of magnanimity—now melted by the tenderness of Birtha, now elevated by the heroism of Ælla? In the parting scene, which is ably managed, the spirit of the warrior predominates over that of the lover; while Birtha, an exquisitely winning pourtrait of female frailty, is carried resistlessly down the stream of her sensations.—**The song of** the minstrel is remarkable for it's simplicity, it's **sweetness and pathos.**

> " Come with a corne-coppe and thorne,
> Drayne mie heartys blodde awaie;
> Lyfe and all yttes goode I scorne,
> Daunce bie nete, or feaste by daie.
>   My love ys dedde,
>   Gon to hys death-bedde
>   All under the wyllow tree.
>   &c. &c."

In "the Fragment of Godwin," the chorus of Freedom would not have disgraced the lyre of Gray. In the battle of Hastings, amid a profusion of similies and metaphors, the exuberance of a juvenile imagination, there are examples of the true sublime. "The Ballad of Charity" cannot be read without tender emotions; for imagination instantly suggests that the wretchedness of the poet, was signified in that of the pilgrim.

To form a true estimate of the genius of Chatterton, we must not forget that the beauties of his poetry, are less resplendent, than they otherwise would be, from the perverted and antiquated diction, and the often barbarous and incongruous idiom, by which they are obscured. Many of the words, used by Chatterton, were the coinage of his own fancy; others are distorted from their common and regular acceptation in ancient writers; and the elegance of modern phraseology is blended with the factitious incrustations of antiquity.

faith; but they say little of vital benevolence; without which faith can be but a sound. How different their

---

The sensations which we experience in perusing some of the best of our ancient poets, are not unlike those which will be felt by a man of a cultivated sensibility, who walks in a Gothic aisle, when the rays of the moon are gleaming on the chambers of the dead; but those which we imbibe from the poetry of Chatterton, though they have less solemnity, have something more of softness, as if we were sitting in an ancient choir, and and were now inspired by the grandeur of the scene—now melted by the sweetness of the harmony.——The genuine poet, is known by the degree of energy, with which he can influence our sensations, and make them respond to his master volition; who powerfully touches the chords of our hearts, and deprives us of the possession of ourselves. A second rate poet only plays about the heart; but a poet of the first order, like Shakespear in many passages and like Chatterton in a few, storms every avenue of the soul; and makes us glow with enthusiasm, or sadden with despair.

The genius of Chatterton languished in the atmosphere of Bristol; his productions were not to the taste of the merchants, who were wallowing in the luxury of wealth; while the poet was suffered to feel the piercing anguish of penury and of scorn. He, accordingly, accepted the offers of some London Booksellers, who invited him to the metropolis. In April, 1770, he left his native city; glowing, probably, with those gay illusions of fame and fortune, with which hope is continually cheating the burning fancy of youth. But the fond expectations of poor Chatterton were never realised; and distracted with the recollection of past neglect, and the prospect of future misery, he took poison on the evening of the 24th of August, 1770, of which he expired the next morning, when he wanted almost three months to complete his eighteenth year.

Far be it from me to become the apologist of self-murder;—but I must say, that when distressed genius (genius, whose sensations are so tremblingly delicate, *and which feels misery with ten times the poignancy of ordinary mortals*), in the bitterness of anguish, shuts out the hope of mercy

discourses from the discourses of Jesus! The instructions of Jesus, combine the purest morals, with calm and sober but solemn devotion. They teach love as the essential principle of piety. They do not found salvation, on the shadowy base of a faith in doctrines which are inscrutable to the wit of man, and equally obscure to the ignorant and the wise.

Mr. Wilberforce, in his View of Christianity, seems to suppose, that a steady and undoubting conviction of the inborn and radical corruption of the human heart, is the foundation-stone of righteousness. In the 12mo. edit. of 1797. p. 18. Mr. Wilberforce says of man,

---

by becoming it's own destroyer, those ought, in some measure, to share the guilt of the crime, who refused the patronage, by which it might have been prevented. Horatio! thou too art descended to the dust of thy fathers, or I should be tempted to say that which would awaken thy remorse!!!

Mr. Warton has observed, that Chaucer is like a genial day, in an English spring; but Chatterton appears to resemble a meteor seen in a summer sky; which passes away too soon for all it's deviations to be noted, or all it's lustre to be ascertained.

To this note I shall only add, that, in the year 1790, I saw the mother and sister of Chatterton. The mother was very infirm and sickly; the sister kept a day-school, and had, I think, one little daughter. They were in indigent circumstances!

that he is " tainted with fin, not flightly and fuperficially, but radically and to the very core." And in p. 32. he fays, " It is here" (*viz.* in the doctrine of the original and innate corruption of mankind) : " never let it be forgotten, *that our foundation muſt be laid; otherwiſe our ſuperſtructure, whatever we may think of it, will one day or other prove tottering and inſecure.*"

It is furely ftrange, that our hopes of falvation muſt be precarious and infecure, before we have debafed our natural fenfe of juftice fo far, as to give a cordial affent to the doctrine of imputed fin. Can any man, in his fenfes, and the exercife of whofe underftanding is not palfied by the dwarfifh cowardice of fuperftition, acquiefce in the notion of inbred and inalienable guilt? Does fin confift, not in finning, but in paffing our mother's womb?

Our mere defcent from Adam, does not make us finful; nor, *till we have ſinned in our own perſons*, can we be worthy objects of divine punifhment. That, as the defcendants of Adam, we are born under a curfe, I can fafely allow; but what is the curfe?—Not, furely, the curse of eternal damnation, or of imputed sin, but the curse of being mortal.—We are all subject to death, which we might not have been, if Adam had not sinned. "Dust thou art, and unto dust thou shalt return," was the curse passed upon Adam, on account of his transgression; and this curse, which was passed on him, is entailed on his latest posterity. Adam, being made mortal, could not certainly transmit immortal energies to those who came after him.

Let us now consider the law, to which Adam was subject in Paradise. He was made immortal on certain conditions; and these conditions were to him a law, which he was bound not to disobey. "Of every tree in the garden," said the Lord to Adam, "thou mayest freely eat; but of the tree of the knowledge of good and evil, thou shalt not eat of it; for, in the day that thou eatest thereof, thou shalt surely die."

As Adam was threatened with death, in case he eat of the forbidden fruit, we must necessarily infer that if he had not eaten of it, he would not have died.—But he had no sooner transgressed the covenant, by adhering to which he might have remained immortal, and exempt from pain and disease, than he became mortal, and subject to those pains and miseries, and various bodily infirmities which are essential to a state of mortality, and which, by wasting the power of the body, hasten it's dissolution. —The consequences, therefore, in which the disobedience of Adam involved his posterity, are these;—pain, disease, and death!

The sentence of eternal damnation, was not only not passed upon Adam and his descendants, but, at the very moment that the sentence of death and the decree of mortality was pronounced against them, a hope was held out to them;—a hope which was, indeed, at first, faint and dubious, but which gradually grew clearer, as the star of Jacob approached the horizon,—that the Almighty would, under the influence of the second Adam, restore the sons of men to those immortal privileges, which they would have possessed, if the first Adam had not sinned.

" I will," said the Lord to the serpent, Gen. iii. 15. " put enmity between thee and the woman, and between thy seed and her seed; and it shall bruise thy head, and thou shalt bruise his heel." Here was an intimation, dark indeed and myſterious, but, not without gleams of ſolace, given to our firſt parents—that they ſhould hereafter, in the perſon of one of their deſcendants, puniſh the ſerpent, by whoſe guile they had been betrayed; and that the wound, under which they languiſhed, ſhould not be incurable. This is not obſcurely ſignified, by the wound itſelf being repreſented as a bruiſe only upon the heel, and not on any vital part.——Thus we ſee that Adam was puniſhed for his tranſgreſſion by temporary ills, and by death, which is itſelf only a temporary ill; but that the conſolatary proſpect of a life after death, and a repeal of the ſentence paſſed on him was dimly ſhadowed forth to him.

How then can it be ſaid, with the leaſt ſhow of truth, that we are by nature, and as it were, in right of our deſcent from Adam, heirs of eternal wrath and worthy of eternal miſery? For we ſee that the ſentence paſſed on Adam himſelf was nothing more than death temporal, and ſhort-lived miſery.

If the conſequences of Adam's tranſgreſſion are entailed on his poſterity, thoſe conſequences may be ſummed up in the mortality of our bodies. " In Adam all die;" as the Apostle said; but to pretend that we are vile and guilty in the sight of God, merely from having been born of Adam (a thing, by the by, which we had no means of preventing), is to assert what is as repugnant to Scripture as it is to reason. It seems, indeed, a downright absurdity, to suppose, with Mr. W. that we are, by nature, necessarily and inherently sinners; that sin has been incorporated in every drop of blood that flows in the heart, and in every fibre that constitutes the tissue of the human frame.

Sin, means a wilful violation of the laws of God; and is the voluntary perversion of that faculty which enables us to distinguish between good and evil. Moral guilt, implies a concomitant consciousness of duty; and where this consciousness is not, as it certainly is not either in infants or ideots, there can be no guilt. Moral depravity, signifies depraved affections and habits of acting; and *which are not innate but acquired.*

To teach people that they are morally and essentially guilty, before they have committed sin, and doomed to eternal punishment, before they have done any thing to deserve any punishment at all, can only tend to give the moſt confuſed notions of moral virtue, to deſtroy the vital ſpirit of human rectitude, and to excite the moſt unworthy ideas of the Supreme Being;—as of a malicious Demon, bringing myriads of ſentient creatures into exiſtence, on purpoſe to torture them to everlaſting ages.

Had the doctrine—that men are by nature ſinners, and that guilt is radical and innate in every heart, been an eſſential part of Chriſtian knowledge, our Saviour would, certainly, have inſiſted on it, as a preliminary to ſalvation; and taught it as the rudiments of immortality. He would have repreſented it as the only rock of Chriſtian ſafety, inſtead of conferring eternal life on thoſe who kept the commandments. Matt. xix. 17. In none of his diſcourſes, did Jeſus inculcate to his followers, the neceſſity of a conviction in the original and radical corruption of human nature, as that only groundwork of piety, " without which, any ſuperſtructure that we might raiſe *would be tottering and inſecure.*" Jeſus ſeems everywhere to conſider men as beings endued with paſſion and with reaſon, and ſuſceptible of good as well as of evil.

The first words in which both Jesus and the Apostles seem to have begun their preaching, were an exhortation to repentance. "Repent ye," was their ordinary exordium. Now, repentance must refer to acquired, not imputed guilt,—that guilt to which the will consented, not that to which it could not be accessary. It would have been madness to require men to repent of that sin which they had no concern in willing; and which was committed many ages anterior to their possession of the faculty of volition.

"I am not," said Jesus, Matt. ix. 13. "come to call the righteous, but sinners to repentance." This implies that there were some who needed no repentance. Had Jesus been an advocate for the doctrine of radical and inherent depravity, he would not have acknowledged that any were righteous; since, in that case, all must have been equally tainted, if not with personal, at least, with imputed guilt. When it was alledged as a charge against Jesus, that he ate with publicans and sinners. "They that be whole," said he, "need no physician but they that are sick." Matt. ix. 12. This passage intimates, that that corruption which Mr. Wilberforce deems universal, and innate in the whole mass of mankind, was only partial to individuals; and, by it's being represented under the image of a sickness, we may suppose that Jesus considered it as rather accidental and acquired, than innate and unavoidable. He seems to have thought the corruption of man rather a secondary than a primary disease; rather a sickness at the extremities than " *at the core;*" rather a local malady, than a total gangrene.

That Jesus did not esteem guilt innate in man, we may, likewise, plainly gather from the concise but impressive eulogy which he pronounced on the *innocence* of little children. " Of *such* is the kingdom of God." He makes the spotless innocence of infancy emblematic of the possessors of the happy mansions. If men are born, as Jesus evidently thought and openly declared, in a state of guiltless innocence, the notion of imputed sin is *a mere chimæra*, which ought no longer to be suffered to throw it's bewildering and terrific gloom over the serene beauty of the Christian system. *

---

* I have dwelt a good deal on this subject; because I am of opinion that thousands and thousands have been prevented from embracing Christianity by the imprudence of divines, in insisting, with so much vehemence,

Let it then, henceforth, pass into the silence of oblivion, along with the numerous corruptions of the true gospel by bigotry and superstition. Let us boldly, but reverently, discreetly and soberly, remove this and other incrustations of time, of ignorance and prejudice from the system of Jesus; and let us display the genuine and unvitiated spirit of his religion to the world;—of that religion which is to be found in a fair and liberal interpretation of his discourses and his actions. This seems the only way of determining with precision what is, and what is not, Christianity.—I am well aware that, in delivering these sentiments, I shall render myself obnoxious to those who love to range, with a certain confusedness of mind, in the dark perplexities of mystery, and forsake the guidance of reason, in the coverts of some inexplicable doctrine.

I do not deny but that texts which seem to favour the doctrine of imputed sin, may be drawn from the

---

on the necessity of assenting to the doctrine of imputed sin—a doctrine which would found Christian morality on a frail and perishable foundation—a doctrine which militates against the general tenor of Scripture, and which is contrary to the most enlarged notions of the Divine Goodness.

writings of St. Paul; but, at the same time, I could produce from the same writings passages of an opposite tendency; and while the epistles of that apostle are so little understood and so liable to inferences, which, perhaps, the Apostle himself never thought of, I think it most safe, as well as wise, in considering any disputed point of doctrine, to confine our attention *solely and exclusively to those points of doctrine which Jesus himself plainly and unequivocally sanctioned by his authority.*

It cannot be denied, that the epistles of St. Paul are interspersed with many useful precepts for the regulation of life and conduct, in the various relations of social intercourse. He sometimes applies the general rules of our Saviour to specific duties. He details the relative obligations of husband and wife, master and servant;— and it ought never to be forgotten, that he has pronounced (1 Cor. xiii.) one of the most comprehensive, beautiful and sublime eulogies on charity, that was ever uttered. Regarding it merely as a specimen of human eloquence, it may vie with the finest passages in the finest productions of Greece or of Rome.

But rules for the conduct of life, or counsels of universal application form, comparatively, but a small part of the writings of Paul. They are, like rays, thinly scattered through an expanse of mysterious darkness. The major part of his epistles is filled with the abstruse discussions of Rabbinical learning; or relates to questions which are, at present, of more curiosity than importance; though, in his time, they interrupted the harmony of the Christian community, and were debated with eagerness, as points which were connected with an eternal interest. But time has both lessened their interest and darkened their meaning.

The Epistle to the Romans is bewildered with the polemical Christianity of that day; and turns on points which were agitated, with no little vehemence, not only between the unbelieving Jews and the Judaizing Christians, but between the latter and the Gentile converts.

The obscurity of the writings of St. Paul is likewise increased by the intricacy of his style; by the long parentheses, which sometimes interrupt the succession of his ideas; and, at others, seems to perplex and confuse the order of his arguments. He likewise so often reasons in the perfon of his adverfary, that it is probable, that notions have often been imputed to Paul, which he rather combated than defended. He seems likewife, at times, to labour with myfterious meanings; and which he failed in developing with fufficient perfpicuity. He was of the fect of the Pharifees, who were wont to allegorife on the literal fenfe of Scripture. His writings have undoubtedly fome tincture of Cabbaliftical refinement; and it may be doubted whether they do not occafionally glimmer with a ray of Grecian philofophy.

The character of Paul was diftinguifhed by intrepidity and energy. It had no littleneffes, no minute or dwarfifh features;—all is force, grandeur and fublimity. He was impatient in purfuit; and indefatigable in exertion. Difdaining obftacles, they rather accelerated than retarded his progrefs. He refembled Cæfar, as characterifed by Lucan:—

"Nil factum reputans dum quid fupereffet agendum."

Previous to his converfion, he was a fierce and inexorable, but a confcientious enemy to Chriftianity. Acts xxvi. Attached, even to bigotry, to the rites of the

Mosaic law, he exhibited an implacable rage against the disciples of Jesus. Not content with persecuting them at Jerusalem, his restless spirit pursued them to other cities, whither they had fled for safety. Acts xxvi.

The honest zeal of Paul was not abated by his conversion; it's direction only was altered. It flowed in a different channel, but with equal impetuosity. Of that religion, against which, he had gone to Damascus, breathing threatnings and slaughter, he became the undaunted, the indefatigable and unshaken advocate.

His natural ferocity was tempered by the gentle spirit of his new master. He no longer gave way to the intemperate ebullition of his passions; he did not thirst for the blood of the unbelieving Jews, as he had formerly done, for that of the believing Christians. He exhibited to the world an illustrious example of Christian piety, dignified by the greatness of it's exertions, and the magnanimity of it's sufferings; and he shewed how the most sublime feelings of devotion are compatible with the diligence of industry, and with the ordinary occupations of life.

The prudent management of Paul was evinced in bringing that heterogeneous mass, which formed the first Christian societies, into a benevolent union. Both the Jew and the Gentile converts were polluted by a thousand diverse superstitions and prejudices; and which must have opposed obstacles to their reciprocal friendship, which nothing but great ability, combined with great moderation, great temper and perseverance, assisted by the divine influence, could have surmounted.

Setting out on his mission to convert the Gentile world—what a dreary and tremendous prospect lay before him! Accumulated dangers pressed on every side.—He had prejudices to vanquish; animosities to soften; he had to elude secret treachery and open force; he had to contend with the machinations of the crafty and with the violence of the powerful.—But from these difficulties he did not shrink, either on account of their variety, their multitude or their danger. He saw the grave before him; but he beheld the star of Jacob rising beyond it's confines.

Death was to him an object of hope and of exultation; but he did not defy it's terrors, like the ambitious enthusiast, impatient for the parade of martyrdom, or because it promised the fading laurels of posthumous fame, but welcomed it's approach because he knew that it would bring him a far more exceeding and eternal weight of glory.

But while I am happy to pay the pious tribute of unfeigned homage to the illustrious Apostle of the Gentiles, I must still adhere to this opinion, which I have entertained almost ever since I have been able to exert the faculty of reflection,—that all the Christianity with which it is necessary for us to be acquainted, is contained, in the Four Gospels and Acts. The same opinion seems to have been held by a great and profound theologian.* " I have a strong persuasion," says Lardner, " that the *gospel was plain at first. It is contained in the Four Gospels and Acts, which are plain books.* If Christianity be not plain now, I apprehend it must be our own fault some how or other."— The fault appears to me to be this—that we do not sufficiently confine our attention to the Gospels, and particularly to the discourses of Jesus, which comprehend

---

* Dr. Lardner. See his Works, vol. i. Lxxxviii.

every necessary article of faith or of practice. Instead of endeavouring to render Christianity plain, too many divines wilfully perplex it with subtleties. They rather labour to puzzle the understanding "*with questions and strifes of words,*" than to inform it with that practical wisdom, " which maketh wise unto salvation."

The discourses of Jesus, which we ought never to lose sight of, when we are discussing any doctrinal or practical points of Christianity, combine the purest morals with calm and sober, but solemn, devotion. They teach love, as the essential principle of piety. They do not found salvation on the shadowy base of a faith in doctrines, which are inscrutable to the wit of man, and equally obscure to the ignorant and the wise.

The divine author of Christianity, instead of wrapping holiness in mystery, and evaporating practical goodness in the flames of enthusiasm,* turned the atten-

---

* The pretended Evangelical preachers, who have found a patron and disciple in Mr. Wilberforce, endeavour to lay what they imagine the foundation stone of righteousness, by convincing their followers of their universal, inbred and radical corruption. An implicit assent to this dogma, they inculcate as the rudiments of religion.—Before they cheer their vota-

tion of his followers to active beneficence; and inculcated that vital morality, which seeks the favour of heaven by increasing the happiness of man.

All the miracles of Jesus, as far as they can be objects of human imitation, are lessons of practical goodness. The power by which they were effected, will be

---

ries with any glad tidings, they take uncommon pains to convince them that the guilt of Adam has eaten into the very cores of their hearts, that they are sinful creatures, and merit, by the destinies of nature, eternal damnation. When their disciples have so far abandoned the use of their reason as to be immersed over head and ears in the absurdity of this doctrine, which they take care to set forth in every image of horror which superstition, hypocrisy and folly, reciprocally operating on each other, can suggest; they then teach the submissive novice, to take refuge in "a *saving faith*;" as, in Popish countries, the vilest miscreants are (or rather *were*) often invited to elude the pursuit of justice in the walls of the sanctuary. On the subject of this "*saving faith,*" the misnamed Evangelical preachers always labour to sublime the sensations of their hearers to a degree of effervescing transport and enthusiasm, far beyond the temperature of common sense and of moral observance. Raised to a pitch of rapture, they imagine that they have nothing more to do than to grasp the crown of glory, though they have, perhaps, neglected every habit of goodness, and all the benign graces of Christian benevolence, to which it is appended. Thus do these men—the wolves in sheeps' cloathing—impose upon the credulity of the illiterate and unthinking part of mankind; and they are often greedily listened to by others, who, *not liking the pains of acquiring moral habits, wish to get to heaven with the least trouble.* They, therefore, enter with alacrity on the cheap and commodious way of "*saving faith.*"

for ever beyond our reach; but we may, without pre-sumption, aspire to catch the spirit of beneficence, that prompted their execution. They tell us, in unequivocal language, to sympathise with wretchedness in all it's varieties.

If we cannot raise the dead man from the bier, can we not administer consolation to the dying, and smooth their passage to the grave? If we cannot make the lame to walk or the blind to see, still life presents us with sufficient opportunities of doing good. Is there not a widow or an orphan left among us? Are we acquainted with none whose strength is wasting away in sickness? with none, who have felt the rude hand of adversity, and, in whose eyes, the ray of hope has been extinguished by misfortune?

In the checquered sorrows of life, in the melancholy vicissitudes of suffering humanity, how many opportunities has the heart of being kind, and the hand of being bountiful? And yet, how often, in a fit, perhaps, of sullenness or disdain, in a moment of cold indifference, or of voluptuous selfishness, do we suffer these opportunities to pass unheeded by us?—But these are opportunities which are more precious than any thing of mere temporal eſtimation, as they are connected with an immortal intereſt; and ought to be regarded as the means which Heaven, whoſe wiſdom may be traced in all it's apparently motley and fortuitous diſpenſations, deſigns to train up man for a ſtate of eternal bleſſedneſs, by habits of love, of gratitude and every tender ſympathy.

The majority of the parables of Jeſus, of which ſome are not more remarkable for uſefulneſs of inference, than for genuine beauty of compoſition, are of a practical tendency. The ſeveral parables of the rich man and Lazarus, Luke xvi. of the Phariſee and the Publican, Luke xviii. of the rich man, who laid up a treaſure for himſelf, and was not rich towards God, Luke xii. of the indigent father and the undutiful ſon, Luke xv. of the merciful maſter and the hard-hearted ſervant, Matt. xviii. of the good Samaritan, Luke x.—all theſe parables inculcate various branches of piety,—of a piety not enthuſiaſtic, vain and illuſory, but fruitful, ſober, intelligible and ſuited to the purpoſes of common life. They tend to ſublime the narrow and ſelfiſh feelings;

and to widen, around the individual, the horizon of mercy and of charity.

The nature of our redemption, by Jesus, has been a subject of much dispute among Christians. Some have entertained such high notions of it's efficacy, as to suppose that no works which we can do, can at all conduce to our salvation.

This doctrine is pregnant with infinite mischief: and were it universally received, would be fatal to the interests of justice and benevolence. But it is abhorrent both to Scripture* and to reason.

---

* " The hour is coming, in the which all that are in the graves shall hear his voice;" (the voice of the son of man;) " and shall come forth;— they that *have done good* unto the resurrection of life, and they that *have done evil* unto the resurrection of damnation." John v. 28, 29.

In St. Matt. xxv. Jesus makes charity the principal ground of acceptance, at the day of Judgment. Knowing the indolent reluctance of many readers to turn to any book that is not before them, and, particularly, when that book happens to be the holy Scriptures, I shall make no apology for transcribing the whole passage to which I allude.

" When the Son of man shall come in his glory, and all the holy angels with him, then shall he sit upon the throne of his glory;—And before him shall be gathered all nations: and he shall separate them one from another, as a shepherd divideth his sheep from the goats: And he shall

There is another opinion, that we are to be made immortal and happy by works only; and without any reference to the conciliatory influence of divine love, manifested in the perfon, and energetically operating in the

---

fet his fheep on his right hand, but the goats on the left. Then fhall the King fay unto thofe on his right hand, Come, ye bleffed of my Father, inherit the kingdom prepared for you from the beginning of the world: For I was an hungered, and ye gave me meat; I was thirfty, and ye gave me drink; I was a ftranger, and ye took me in: Naked, and ye clothed me; I was fick, and ye vifited me; I was in prifon, and ye came unto me.—Then fhall the righteous anfwer, faying, Lord, when faw we thee an hungered, and fed thee? or thirfty, and gave thee drink? When faw we thee a ftranger, and took thee in? or naked, and clothed thee? or when faw we thee fick or in prifon, and came unto thee? And the King fhall anfwer, and fay unto them, Verily, I fay unto you, inafmuch as ye have done it unto one *of the leaft of thefe, my brethren, ye have done it unto me.* —Then fhall he fay, alfo, unto them on his left hand, Depart from me, ye curfed, into everlafting fire, prepared for the devil and his angels. For I was an hungered, and ye gave me no meat? I was thirfty, and ye gave me no drink; I was a ftranger, and ye took me not in; naked, and ye clothed me not; fick and in prifon, and ye vifited me not. Then fhall they alfo anfwer him, faying, Lord, when faw we thee an hungered, or athirft, or a ftranger, or naked, or fick, or in prifon, and did not minifter unto thee? Then fhall he anfwer them, faying, Verily, I fay unto you, inafmuch as ye did it not unto one of the leaft of thefe, ye did it not to me. And thefe fhall go away into everlafting punifhment; but the righteous into life eternal."———No part of Scripture is more diftinct and definite than this is. It admits of no equivocations; it is fo clear that he " who runs may read;" and it deferves the ferious confideration of thofe perfons, who, trufting to the enthufiaftic fumes of imagination, think that there is a fafer way to heaven than that of benevolence.

atonement of Jesus. The truth, in this case, as in many others, seems to be placed between the extremes of the opposite opinions. It appears to me, that of the eternal life which the Scriptures promise to mankind, the mediatorial sacrifice of Christ is the essential cause, and benevolence the qualifying habit.

Immortal happiness is the free gift of God; it is not a debt paid to justice nor a tribute to merit. Nor is it a forced gift. We may either accept it or refuse it. If we accept it, we must prove our acceptance an act of rational choice, and, at the same time, of grateful remembrance, by conforming to the conditions to which it is appended.

Eternal happiness is a covenanted mercy. If we will enter life, we must keep the commandments; we must live in obedience to the precepts of the gospel: but still this obedience does not, in the least degree, merit immortality. It is no equivalent, no satisfaction paid to the Almighty for so high a privilege. This still remains the free-will offering of divine mercy, influenced by divine love.

The necessity of obedience does not at all invalidate the excellence of the free gift; it rather increases it, by fitting our natures for it's enjoyment. The parent, who leaves his child an inheritance, subject to conditions, of which the performance tends only to encrease the enjoyment, is not surely less but more bountiful on that account. The very restrictions he imposes are acts of kindness and proofs of love.—The conditions of the gospel ought to be considered in this light. These conditions may be summed up in one word, but of very extensive signification,—in Charity. Charity does not merely imply benevolent acts, but benevolent thoughts and affections: in one word, Christian charity denotes a heart filled with that sacred stream of divine love which overflows in love to mankind. This is that qualifying habit, which I mentioned above; and which divine mercy made a condition of future happiness; because it tends to approximate us to the image of God; and because we could not be happy, even in heaven, without it.

Jesus makes a happy immortality, as far as it is an act of a man's own choice, to consist in benevolence;* though he refers the gift itself, not to our merits, but to the mere mercy of God, through the mediatorial sacrifice of the Son, whose " birth was of the womb of the morning;"—" whose goings forth were from of old, from everlasting."†

If the unbeliever ask me, How, and in what precise manner the sacrifice of Jesus could annul the mortality of the human species, and procure for mankind an admission into mansions of eternal blessedness, I must fairly confess that I cannot explain it. It is enough for us to know, that we cannot be fitted for those mansions, without becoming like unto Jesus, in our benevolent affections. It it enough for us, if we have adequate

---

* See the passage which I have quoted from St. Matt. page 139, 140.

† Jesus represents himself as the source of immortality, in the following passages. " I am the way, the truth and the life; no man cometh unto the father but by me. John xiv. 6. " I am the living bread which came down from heaven: if any man eat of this bread he shall live for ever; and the bread that I will give is my flesh, which I will give for the life of the world." In a solemn invocation to his Father, a little before his agony in the garden, Jesus says, " *This is life eternal, that they might know thee, the only true God; and Jesus Christ whom thou hast sent.* John xvii. 3.

conceptions and a serious conviction of this truth, without perplexing the mind to unravel mysteries, which can never be comprehended, and *which heaven never designed that man should comprehend.* In a future life, more pages of the book of revealed, as well as natural knowledge, will probably be unfolded to us: at present, there are many inexplicable points in both; on which, while our faculties are thus dim, it behoves us to be silent.

If, knowing our duty here, we perform it to the best of our power, we shall certainly be accepted of God. Whether we square our faith by the precepts of Athanasius, or Arius, or Socinus, we shall enter into life, if we keep the commandments; and follow, as nearly as possible, the steps of Jesus, which point the way to immortality.* Vainly to attempt to pierce the

---

* I feel a firm, unshaken conviction, that it is the vital benevolence of the heart and affections, and not the mere assent of the mind to any mystery of doctrine, which constitutes that religion which is most pleasing in the sight of God. There cannot be a more concise and just description of religion than that by St. James i 2, 7. "Pure religion and undefiled before God and the Father is this; To visit the poor and fatherless in their affliction, and to keep himself unspotted from the world."

clouds and darkness that surround the Christian sanctuary may waste our time, but cannot improve our piety. To meditate on things that are above the sphere of our comprehension, and on which, if we lived for a thousand years we could never form any distinct ideas, only serves to bewilder the understanding, without mending the heart. The religion of Jesus consists more in beneficent actions than in contemplative raptures;—more in the calm and serene sensations of meekness, gentleness and forgiveness than in the wild emotions of enthusiasm.

That this is a faithful delineation of the spirit of the religion of Jesus, we may easily learn from an attentive perusal of his various discourses; and particularly his inimitable sermon on the mount; which is a summary of the whole Christian doctrine; and which exhibits a picture of mild, unostentatious piety, softening the affec-

---

There are, certainly, good and bad men among all sects; and, perhaps, it would be difficult to say, on which side the sum of moral worth preponderates. Hence, ought we not to learn that what opinions we entertain about certain dark and inexplicable matters, are not essential to salvation? And ought they to kindle any animosity between us? Ought we to behold the mote in our brother's eye, and to neglect the beam in our own?—HOW LONG WILL *Christians continue* TO HATE EACH OTHER?

tions, purifying the thoughts, and infusing into the soul the sacred fire of pure, undefiled devotion; and of love human and divine.

In Jesus there was a warm and exalted spirit of devotion. In prayer he seems to have passed the intervals that were left to him from the exercise of charity, and the functions of his public ministry.

The Evangelists frequently tell us of his retiring to a mountain to pray.* St. Luke vi. 12. tells us—" that Jesus went out to a mountain, where he continued all night in prayer to God." Retiring from the bustle of the world, he sought to give vent to the emotions of piety, in the tranquillity of solitude. He went where he might not be disturbed by the " busy hum of men."

The shades of silence and of solitude are certainly most congenial to those exercises of devotion; from which, man returns into the world with fresh energy to combat it's pollutions, and to resist it's temptations.

---

* See Matt. xiv. 13. John vi. 15.

The example, as well as the instructions, of Jesus* enjoin us, occasionally, to quit the intercourse of society, in order to commune with our own hearts and with him who made us. In this hallowed commerce, the soul, as it were, breaths in a purer atmosphere; where it's organs, refined from their grossness, expand with a more free and spiritual energy.

The spirit of devotion, whose habitual exercise feeds and keeps alive it's own flame, is soon chilled into torpor or weakened into lassitude, by continued and unremitting converse with the gay and busy world.

No man's heart is proof against the seductions of unceasing dissipation. Unless the thoughts are turned by frequent abstraction from temporal and sensual objects, and purified by the fire of the altar, they soon

---

* "And in the morning, rising up a great while before day, he went out and departed into a solitary place, and there prayed," Mark i. 35.

"When thou prayest, thou shalt not be as the hypocrites are; for they love to pray standing in the synagogues and in the corners of the streets, that they may be seen of men. But thou, when thou prayest, enter into thy closet, and when thou hast shut the door, pray to thy Father which is in secret." &c. Matt. vi. 5, 6.

degenerate into filth and corruption. An occasional sequestration from the world is necessary to liberate us from the force of it's enchantments.

The heart of man is naturally disposed to what is good;* virtue and beneficence seem most congenial to to it; they please without any factitious charms; but as it is, on all sides, accessible to temptations, corruption soon finds a way into it.—To guard against corruption, it becomes necessary to cultivate the spirit of devotion; which, when it has become habitual, when God our father, and Jesus, his messenger of immortality, are the objects of our warmest affections and our often-contem-

---

* I am not ignorant, that many are of opinion, that the heart of man is *naturally more* disposed to evil than to good.—But moral evil appears as repugnant to his natural sentiments, as pain or physical evil is to his natural feelings.

Moral and physical good have a more intimate connection than is generally supposed. It is not improbable, that man is born with a moral, as well as a physical taste; but both are liable to be vitiated by improper management, and perverse associations. Thus the moral taste comes to relish cruelty and injustice; as the physical taste, by the same sort of aberration from it's natural and healthy state, is brought to find a gratification in alcohol and tobacco, and a thousand nauseous and unwholesome drinks and viands.

plations, the fascination of perishable pleasures is broken, and reason rises superior to the tyranny of the senses.

From the shrine of devotion, we gather strength to advance in holiness. If our affections are soured by the injuries of enemies or the treachery of friends, prayer is a sovereign balm to assuage the fretful acrimony of the heart. In the holy effusions of prayer, the spirit of animosity is exhaled into a diviner element; and we imbibe courage to imitate Jesus in doing good; careless whether the good we do, meet with imprecations or with praises.

Our prayers to God ought to be associated with fervor and with seriousness. When we are on the knees of devotion, we should steadily keep our thoughts fixed on the Divine Presence; and should never forget, that God knows all we think, as well as all we say. To be guilty of levity, in any work of moment, shews littleness of mind;—but to suffer any levity to debase our worship of the Almighty, is to mingle folly with impiety.

In his acts of religious adoration, Jesus seems, as far

as we can collect from the short notices of the Evangelists, to have been, in a most peculiar manner, distinguished by earnestness and solemnity. The characteristic fervency of his devotional exercises may be seen by consulting John xvii. which contains a sublime, a feeling and impressive intercession to his heavenly father for his disciples and followers; and which well describes the awful and dignified seriousness of his devotion.

Before his apprehension, Jesus retired to prepare for the last hour of his stay among mortals, in the shades of the garden of Gethsemane. What warmth, what sincerity, what energy of piety is marked in his prayer, at that distressing moment! " Father! if thou be willing, remove this cup from me; nevertheless, not my will, but thine be done!" This prayer does not lose it's emphasis by it's concisenefs. Genuine anguish is never diffusive. It is more given to taciturnity or abruptness than to prolixity. This prayer of Jesus will suit every Christian, who, languishing in sorrow, lifts up his head to heaven, for that comfort which nothing in the world can bestow.

Devotion is that fountain, from which misery may

fetch the purest streams of consolation. The Evangelist tells us, that the prayer of Jesus brought an angel from heaven, to minister comfort unto him. This seems to intimate the power of devotion;—of devotion warm, genuine and sincere. Angels of consolation, though invisible to our perceptions, are probably ever attendant on the righteous; and whisper the spirit of peace, in the inquietude of grief.

The earnestness with which Jesus prayed increased with his increasing despondency. The Evangelist, without any embellishment of rhetoric, tells us, that " he prayed more earnestly;" and he has delineated the exquisite peculiarity of his agonies, by saying, that " his sweat was, as it were, great drops of blood, falling down to the ground."

There is a principle of satiety attached to all earthly objects; the heart soon grows tired of them. It seeks for something imperishable on which to fix. The very organization of man, renders him incapable of unmixed and continued satisfaction in what is sensual and transitory.

The soul will, at times, languish with weariness, in the midst of every human enjoyment. The palled sense and the sick heart seek where to find rest; but they find none here; where they behold every thing in a state of uncertainty, of change and decay. They therefore turn for solace to him who is immutable. The power that made all things becomes the subject of our adoration, the theme of our wonder, our gratitude and our praise.

But we must take care that we do not substitute prayer, which ought to be considered only as an incentive to, for the practice of religious duties. Devotion ought in us, as in Jesus, to be resorted to, not to supplant, but to fill up the interstices of practical piety.

That alone is devotion, true and undefiled, which disposes the heart to the production of human happiness; or makes it sympathise more tenderly with human misery. For this purpose, prayer will first quench in us, all ill-will and animosity towards all men; for, devotion can be no better than idle mummery, if it be not associated with the spirit of mildness and forgiveness.

Before the heart can glow with that genuine love of God which prayer fuppofes, and of which it breaths the fragrant incenfe, every fpark of malevolence towards our fellow-creatures muft be extinguifhed. Without this, prayer, inftead of being an offering fweet and grateful to heaven, is only a fetid vapour, exhaled from corruption.

Prayer extinguifhes hate, in order to kindle love; and the love, that is thus kindled, will not be narrow and partial, limited by exceptions, or debafed by any alloy of bitternefs, but, like the fource from which it flows, and which is the afpiration of the Spirit of God upon the foul, in it's abftraction from all low and perifhable purfuits, it will embrace the expanfe of univerfal nature.

Prayer, while it warms and invigorates all the fympathies which intereft us in the happinefs of our family or our friends, at the fame time, infpires in the breaft the flame of univerfal benevolence. The human race, that are fpread over the whole globe, are the object of Chriftian prayer.—The nearer approaches which the foul makes to it's great and glorious original, the more it inhales the spirit of a diffusive tenderness. It ceases to feel any little vulgar animosities. The flame of divine love, excited in the human breast by the genuine fervor of prayer, exalts and refines all the affections, and makes every nerve of man thrill with the mild and delicious raptures of universal benevolence.

So strenuously does Christianity insist on that piety which is uncontaminated by hypocrisy, that it makes even the government of the thoughts a point of religious duty. On this occasion, it was well said by Boerhave, as the judicious Paley has before remarked, "That our Saviour knew mankind better than Socrates." Impure ideas administer poison to virtue; and food to depravity. They taint the modesty of youth; and they heat the sensuality of age. They injure those decencies which are essential to purity of manners; and that delicacy which is the charm of mixed society. Licentious ideas and licentious discourse, habitually indulged, dissever those combinations of chaste and serious thought which are the defence of virtue; and inevitably lead to a fatal and incurable corruption. "Let no corrupt communication proceed out of thy mouth," was the injunction of divine wisdom; and the integrity of the moral principle depends greatly on it's observance. *

But let it not be supposed, that Christianity is an enemy to the pleasures of innocence, to cheerfulness of converse, and the sparkling gaieties of fancy. The religion of Jesus does not, as men of gloomy minds have too often imagined, direct us to be constantly depressed with despondency, meditating on eternity, or musing over the grave. Are all the energies of man, who is

---

* Count Rumford, vol 1. 35. says, "So great is the effect of cleanliness upon man, that it extends even to his moral habits. Virtue never dwelt long with filth and nastiness; nor do I believe that there ever was a person, scrupulously attentive to cleanliness, who was a consummate villain."

If outward filth and nastiness of body have such an influence on the moral principle, surely a stronger influence must be exerted by filth and nastiness of thought and speech. There is a constant action and reaction between words and ideas. Thus corruption operates with a double force. It is revolting, to observe, in the conversation of the dissolute, the number of harmless and often sacred expressions, which they associate with indecency, and which are no sooner uttered than they kindle the sensual fire. If the young wish to guard against depravity, or the old to stop it's progress, they cannot too scrupulously shun impurity of thought and speech. It may be laid down as a maxim, justified by general experience,—That there is no person, who is habitually foul-mouthed, whose esteem is worth seeking, or whose honesty can be relied on.

said to have been created in the image of God, to be damped by inceſſant reflection on his latter end? Are languor of ſoul and uneaſineſs of conſcience, dejection of ſpirit and gloomineſs of ideas the eſſential characteriſtics of Chriſtian piety? Can we not be ſaved, unleſs we are continually darkening the imagination with the ſufferings of the croſs? Did Jeſus direct that piety which borders on miſanthropy; which, in the deluſive dreams of enthuſiaſm, beſtows the tribute of ſalvation rather on the fervor of the lips, than of the heart; on the auſterity of the devotions, more than on the benevolence of the conduct? Did not Jeſus himſelf ſanction both by precept and example that piety which mingles with the world, without mingling in it's corruptions, or partaking in it's crimes; which neglects not the various duties of public and domeſtic life; and which is the kind promoter of ſocial happineſs in all it's varieties? Did Jeſus reprobate thoſe inoffenſive gaieties of heart, which form a part, and no inconſiderable part, of the captivations of life? Did he repreſent the Chriſtian temper of a gloomy aſpect, covering the face of it's votaries with tears and mourning? Is he not himſelf conſtantly deſcribed in Scripture by the image of a lamb?— an image of cheerfulneſs, which we ought not to diſſociate from our ideas of religion. Is not the kind notice which he took of little children, of whom the characteristic feature is gay and harmless mirth; and his declaration, that of such is the kingdom of God, a sufficient testimony, that he wished rather to increase than to diminish the pleasurable sensations of life; and that the disposition and the manners of a Christian should not be shrouded by the forbidding gloom, the sullen spirit, and the weeping countenance of an enthusiast or a sectary? Is not the first miracle that he wrought, at a marriage, in Cana of Galilee, a declaration that he did not come to banish cheerfulness from the earth; and that the profession of his religion was by no means incompatible with social enjoyment?——Those who sketch the figure of Christianity with a desponding look, and a dejected posture, must be strangers to it's genuine spirit, shedding joy upon the heart, and banishing sadness and asperity from the brow.

At the close of the eighteenth century, let us not rake from it's ashes the spirit of Calvin, scowling with the moroseness of fanaticism;—for ever lowering over the infernal abyss, and scattering fire and brimstone in the paths of harmless pleasantry.—Let us not conjure up this spirit from it's repose, in order to eclipse the spirit of Jesus, bright, serene, unclouded, benign and cheerful; indulgent to human frailty; comforting the weary and the heavy-laden;—friendly to innocent pleasure, and adverse to that sensual apathy and that haggard superstition, which would strip vivacity of it's playfulness and sprightliness of it's smile.

The general complexion of human life is sufficiently melancholy, without any artificial expedients to cover it with more dismal hues. It is a more necessary and more sacred duty to seek for balm, with which to sooth the afflicted, than for sorrows, with which to depress the happy. If we plant the cypress and other emblems of grief among the habitations of the dead, there is no reason why we should not permit the voice of gladness to be heard in the chambers of the living.

There are some recreations which the Puritans of the last century considered as flagrant sins. Among these, the amusements of the drama were more particularly the objects of their invective.

Mr. Wilberforce, whose work is shaded with the

sombre tints of Puritanism, seems to consider the theatres as inauspicious to piety; and as places to which a Christian ought not to resort.

If Mr. Wilberforce do not choose to be present at a play, because the play-houses are frequented by debauchees, he might, on the same ground of argument, abstain from the senate or the sanctuary. Corruption and depravity are to be met with in every walk of life; and under almost every modification of social intercourse; and if we will go where they are not, we must go out of the world at once. I know no other alternative.— But does not Mr. Wilberforce recollect, that the divine author of Christianity eat, without scruple, *at the same table*, with publicans and sinners? Does he not know that virtue is proved by resisting temptation; and that he discovers the brightest integrity who is chaste amid seduction, and incorrupt amid corruption.

The corruptions, of which Mr. Wilberforce complains, are accidental not essential to the theatre; and it is probable that they would exist, with more criminal aggravations, if there were not a theatre in London.— Vice and licentiousness, ingenious in expedients, would soon find other haunts; and which would only be more dangerous if they were more inveloped in the shades of mystery, and less exposed to that influence of public opinion, of which notwithstanding it's partial eccentricities, the general result is always favourable to the interests of virtue, of delicacy and of chastity.

The motive which prompts the amusements of mankind, is agreeable sensation; which admits of two divisions, into physical and moral. The former is suited more to mere animal, the last to rational beings. It cannot be doubted to which class the pleasures of the theatre belong; they are certainly more attached to intellect than to sensuality; and have rather a moral than a physical taste.

The stage, even in it's present degenerate state, when it abandons the sublime efforts of tragedy, which instructs by painting the influence of the passions on the human character and on human happiness, for the wit, the vivacity and the playfulness of comedy, for the drollery of farce, or for the magnificence of dress and scenery, for the pomp of processions and all the ingenious versatility of art,—must still be considered as providing harmless repast;—and one, indeed, of no inconsiderable utility, as it prevents the spectator from recurring to more sensual and pernicious entertainments, to the excesses of the tavern, the discontent and acrimony of the card-table, and the more ruinous criminality of the gaming-house.

It cannot be denied, but that it has been long the fashion, and which has lately grown to a rank excess, to contaminate the language of the drama, with a mixture of ribaldry and obscenity; and a profusion of all the contemptible equivocations of indecency. For these, no excuse can be pleaded; they tend directly to corrupt the heart, and to vitiate the moral sentiments. They profane the sacredness of modesty; and they wither that nice sensibility to the blush of shame, which, when on particular occasions it shews it's delicate tints on the cheek of youth and beauty, is inexpressibly captivating. *

---

* I cannot, in this place, refrain from making a quotation from Dr. Thornton's Medical Extracts,—a work not more conspicuous for it's elegance, than for it's piety; and which deserves a place in the library of every divine, as well as every physician.

The morals of mankind seem reciprocally to influence and to be influenced by their amusements. One gives a colour to the other. This is perhaps the reason why, in London, which is a vast focus of sensuality, so many of our modern productions are so lavishly tinctured with indecency. Depraved morals seek, with curious solicitude, the depraved seasoning of an obscene and wanton phraseology; and which, in it's turn, aggravates the depravity from which it springs.

The only substantial remedy for the corruptions of the theatre, is an amelioration of morals; and which

---

" *Modesty* is one of the most distinguishing and *attractive* characteristics of the female sex. *Modesty* has a double effect : it heightens the desire of the male, and deters him from rudeness, or improper behaviour. It both *attracts* and *repels*. There is no part of the female character which men revere so much as *modesty*. It is the brightest and most valuable jewel with which a woman can be adorned. A fine woman, without *modesty*, instead of gaining the affections of men, becomes an object of contempt. It is, therefore, not only the interest of females to cultivate *modesty*, but to guard, with the most anxious attention, against the smallest encroachments. Every attack, however apparently insignificant, should be repelled with spirit and intrepidity. To men of sensibility, a single glance of the eye will tell them that their conduct is improper, and make them not only instantly desist, but prevent any further attempt. It is equally the interest of men to cherish, and not to injure by indelicacy, a quality from which they derive so much pleasure and advantage." Med. Ext. vol. iii. 512.

would by no means be promoted by the suppression of all theatrical diversions. This effect is only to be hoped for, from a more general and virtuous system of education; and the exhibition *of a purer example* by the great;—the corruption of whose sentiments, the prodigality of whose vices, and the pollution of whose taste descends to those beneath them. At present, the upper ranks are the patrons and the originals of the great mass of folly, indecency and depravity, which are seen not only on the mimic stage, but also on the stage of real life.

But, notwithstanding all the corruptions of the theatre, I am inclined to believe, that when all the means, whether direct or indirect, by which they foster the growth of vice have been computed, a great balance will remain in favour of their general tendency to promote the interests of virtue.

The sympathetic principle, which presides in the breast of the spectator, seems to be always most powerfully excited when virtue is seen to triumph over vice; and when benevolence, full of life and energy, is delineated scattering joy and happiness over the whole extent of it's horizon.—Then, even corruption, for a moment, soaring from it's baseness, pays it's homage to virtue;—then the applauses of the audience are most redoubled and most sincere.

Mr. Wilberforce makes religion to consist in the exercise of the affections; or, in what, according to his description of the matter, and notwithstanding all his palliations, must be understood to mean—an inflamed state of the devotional feelings. Thus he, indirectly, encourages enthusiasm and hypocrisy; for, by artificial contrivances, the affections may be raised to almost any pitch; and the greatest sinners have sometimes been absorbed in what might thus be called—pious ecstacies. The effervescence of devotional feelings has indeed often been the characteristic of the most worthless of mankind.

Mr. Wilberforce would have acted more wisely, if he had made religion to consist, as Jesus Christ evidently did, in those benevolent sympathies which invariably lead to benevolent actions. Here there is no room for hypocrisy or delusion. Religion is appreciated by a rule of which we cannot mistake the application.

When Jesus was asked, which was the great commandment in the law, he answered, "Thou shalt love the Lord thy God with all thy heart, and with all thy soul, and with all thy mind. This the first and great commandment. And the second is like unto it. Thou shalt love thy neighbour as thyself. On these two commandments hang all the law and the prophets." Matt. xxii. In Mark xii. he declared, There is none other commandment greater than these.

Hence we learn, that the love of God, to be pure and holy, must be identified with the love of mankind. In other words—divine love, is social love impelling to pure beneficence; His bosom, therefore, possesses the genuine principle of divine love; the elementary flame of immortal happiness, whose actions and affections are consonant to this grand and fundamental law of all religion and all morality; " Thou shalt love thy neighbour as thyself;" or, as the same precept has been expressed by Jesus, in other words, " Whatsoever ye would that men should do unto you, do ye also unto them." Matt. vii. 12.

Thus we see that the Christian system blends religion

and morality in an indissoluble union. The neglect of one is the neglect of both. To disjoin devotion and morals, or morals and devotion, is to renounce the gospel.

" Thou shalt love thy neighbour as thyself;" is, as we have seen, that command which the founder of Christianity represented, as comprehending the sum of it's duties. The purest adoration, therefore, which we can pay to God, is to promote the happiness of our brethren. Where divine love is made the motive to social, the narrow and selfish vanish in the expanded stream of benevolent sensations. Christian love, glowing warm and genuine in the heart, consumes the force of the selfish principle; as the rod of Aaron swallowed up the rods of the magicians. Exod. vii 12.

There is in man both a selfish and a social principle, —a principle which attaches him to self-interest, and another which binds him to the interests of his kind. The first is encouraged by solitude; which soon compresses the affections into one point, and reconciles the heart to that, of which the social principle inspires the aversion;—the taste of undivided, unshared and isolated enjoyment.

It is the social principle, which, by an invisible but powerful magic, touching all the chords of sympathy, tends to make man weary and comfortless when alone. It attracts him, by an irresistible charm, into an intercourse with his kind, and insinuates an attractive fondness for the endearments of friendship.

Man is placed, in life, in such circumstances and amid such relations as tend to invigorate and expand the social and sympathetic, and to stifle and counteract the selfish principle. The kindred affections, the spirit of family-love, of love parental, filial, fraternal tends to cherish, and unfold, at a very early period, the embryon beauties of benevolent sensation. Even from the breast of our mother we seem to imbibe those benign influences of sympathy which abate the relish for solitary enjoyment, and teach us that we increase our own happiness when we share it with others.

As we grow up, the connections of friendship and of love (particularly the latter), promote still farther the growth of the social principle. Love teaches us that we are most happy by a reciprocation of happiness.

Friendship multiplies the tender links of sympathy; and relaxes the power of selfishness; by associating a multitude of divided interests and sensations with our own.

In Paradise, it was not good for man to be alone; and certainly in that state of complicated misery to which we are born, and in which we have to live, it cannot be good for us to be alone. The fading spirits require the refreshing intercourse of society.

Short intervals of absence from the peopled world, are, indeed, auspicious to virtue; but continued and habitual solitude chills the bosom against the warm impulses of benevolence, and freezes the best blood, that the sympathetic affections would circulate through the heart.

The relations in which nature has placed us and the affections of family, of love and friendship which are the source of so much happiness, and which indeed are the purest sources of human happiness, all tend to elicit and mature the sympathetic principle; which connects the interest of the individual with the interest of his fellow-creatures. By rendering benevolence the source of our most agreeable sensations, they impel to it's exercise, by the most powerful incitement.

Yet, so strongly is the benevolent counteracted by the domineering, selfish principle, that, notwithstanding all the natural and associated causes, which give a bias to benevolence, selfishness too often prevails over sympathy. The love of solitary and exclusive absorbs, instead of being absorbed by, the love of communicated bliss. The individual consults his own happiness, coldly negligent of that of his kindred and his kind. A base and ignominious self-interest becomes the tyrant of the soul, and smothers every spark of benevolent sensation.

But the Christian religion, originating from divine wisdom, and favouring those relations of nature and those attractions of sympathy, which it had before ordained, lends it's awful sanctions to extinguish the selfish and to inspire the social flame.

The messenger of immortality has threatened the selfish with this awful sentence: "Go, ye cursed, into everlasting fire;" while those tender-hearted persons, who, feeling the divine glow of love unfeigned, labour, like ministering angels, to sooth the diversified miseries of human life, shall be called "the blessed of God;" and, when all the grandeur of the world is crumbled into dust, shall shine like the stars for ever and ever.

Thus we see that the whole sum and substance of religion, consists not in the effervescing sensations of devotional zeal, but in the exercise of those benevolent sympathies which endear men to God, while they endear them to each other. Let us constantly try the Christianity of Christans by this test, and we shall never be deceived.

But, if we make religion to consist in those tumultuous emotions of the soul, which have no relation to beneficence, or in a bare assent to those doctrines which have no influence on human conduct, we are only opening a door, by which enthusiasm and imposture may enter into the sanctuary of the righteous, and usurp the honours which belong to sincere and unaffected piety.

But though I am an enemy to enthusiastic zeal, and fanatic turbulence, yet, let it not be supposed, that I would, by any means, discourage that degree of devout sensation, which is the never-failing associate of true holiness; which is mingled with beneficence, and is restrained from the ebullitions of intemperance.

In the breast of the righteous, there is a pure and perenial spring of consolatory sensation, whose waters are never turbid; which, in affliction, are a cordial to the faint spirits; and which, in the torturing hour of misfortune and despondency, cheer the aching breast, with those calm and delicious instillations of love and hope which are a foretaste of immortality.

As far as all the varied emotions of the heart, of which some branch from physical sensibility, others from early association can be preserved separate from the indistinct fervours of enthusiasm, and be made subservient to the energies of practical goodness, they ought to be encouraged.

Of all the affections, of a religious caft, which can enter into the foul of man, gratitude is one which ought to be cultivated with moft care, and cherifhed with moft fondnefs.—Gratitude, which may be denominated, one of the handmaids of practical piety, means fuch a devout and ferious fenfe of the goodnefs of God, as naturally foftens and expands the heart towards his creatures.

When the grateful man receives any diftinguifhed favour or kindnefs from one of his fellow-men, his heart inftantly vibrates towards him with a degree of partial fondnefs. He feels a warm intereft in his benefactor's welfare; he is ready to rejoice over his good fortune, or to mourn over his bad;—and thefe kind emotions are gradually extended towards his family and his connections. His gratitude caufes him, in fome meafure, to identify his own feelings with thofe of his benefactor; he grows attached to his friendfhips, he catches the complexion of his fympathies.

Gratitude to God, where felt in it's genuine purity, will be analogous in it's operations, with gratitude to man; but, in the former, the fenfations of love will be heightened by thofe of adoration. The grateful heart, in it's moments of abstraction from earthly to heavenly objects, thrilling with pure and simple, not riotous and turbid, ecstacies,—will be warmly and affectionately disposed towards the whole family of mankind.

All those tender and sympathetic obligations which we now include in the name of Gratitude, seem, in scriptural language, to be comprehended in the name of Love; and I have before observed, that love to God, is the sum of Christian duty; and comprehends every branch of practical beneficence.

The Apostle John, who was himself a pattern of the meekness of love, in his first epistle, which breaths the spirit of his master, constantly considers love, or gratitude, or whatever affection or species of adoration it be, which divine love embraces, as analogous to practical beneficence.

Our Saviour himself frequently inculcated the same doctrine. In John xiv. 15. he says, " If ye love me, keep my commandments:" again, " He that hath my commandments and keepeth them, he it is that loveth me." These expressions imply an inviolate union between devotion and practical piety—the piety of the affections and the conduct; as will plainly appear when we come to consider what is the substance of those commandments of Jesus; of which, he considers the observance as a full and satisfactory expression of our love to him, or to him that sent him. *

In John xv. 12. Jesus says, with great emphasis, " This is my commandment; that ye love one another, as I have loved you." In John xiii 34, 35. Jesus had enforced this precept, if possible, with more energy; " A *new commandment* I give unto you—that ye love one another; as I also have loved you, that ye love one another. *By this shall all men know that ye are my disciples, if ye have love one to another.*"

Here it is remarkable, that the duty of that mutual love, which St. Paul calls charity, is said to be " a *new commandment.*"—Now, it was not new as to the expression; for the same commandment is found in the law. " Thou shalt love thy neighbour as thyself."

---

* " He that honoureth not the Son, honoureth not the Father who sent him."

Levit. xix. 18.—But, under the Old Testament-dispensation, this rule of life was buried under a mass of ceremonies; and was not made the prominent and distinguishing feature of the Mosaic system.—On the other hand, Jesus insisted on it as the essential characteristic of his disciples; as the test, the pass-word of his religion. He made it a sacred rule of conscience, a vital principle of action; from which all the Christian virtues ought to flow in copious streams; and to dispense happiness, in whatever channel they are rolled.

Well, therefore, might Jesus call this *"a new commandment;* when he enforced it with new energy, consecrated it with new sanctions, and made the spirit of love as essential to the vitality of the Christian system, as the spirit of animation is to the animal functions.

"By this," said the son of man (and let his words sink deep into the heart of every Christian), "shall all men know that ye are my disciple, *if ye have love* ONE TO ANOTHER."—My God! if mutual love be the essential and characteristic distinction of the true followers of Jesus, how long has it been unknown, or how much has it been despised!

The annals of ecclesiastical history, dropping blood and breathing animosity in almost every page, teach us that Christians have been usually more distinguished by their bitterness and asperity, than by their love and forbearance towards each other; and that they have sometimes disgraced the benign religion of their master, by the perpetration of cruelties, at which reason blushes, and benevolence turns pale.

How often has bigotry, whose blood rages with the lust of cruelty, presumed that Christ would be gratified by tying heresy to the stake, or putting it to the sword? Has not the least difference in the merest minutiæ of opinion, in matters of total indifference, or in questions about inscrutable mysteries and inexplicable doctrines, frequently excited the most furious contentions in the Christian world?—contentions which could only be appeased by the slaughter of those among whom they were agitated, and who ought to have been endeared to each other by a reciprocal affection.

It has, alas! but too long been forgotten by those, who have professed the warmest zeal for the religion of Jesus, that *brotherly love ought to be a common bond of harmony and friendship, among all sects and denominations of Christians.* The various shades and complexions of faith, that are found among Christians, ought no more to affect their mutual good-will and kindness, than the earth is affected by the tints or shapes of the ever-changing clouds that sprinkle the horizon.

Whatever may be our differences of opinion about modes of faith, or mysteries of doctrine, we are all equally dear to our common master, Christ; if we fulfil his royal law, and *have love to one another.* By this test, thou hast promised, O blessed Jesus! to own us for thy disciples,—*if we have love one to another.*

Love is the hallowed flame which should be exhaled to heaven, pure as the purest incense from the hearts of Christians. Like the vestal fire, it ought never for a moment to be extinguished. While love prevails, the spirit of Jesus sways the heart; but as soon as it vanishes in the gusts of hate, or the rage of intolerance, the life, the soul, the beauty of Christianity is no more!—The name of Christian may still be usurped, the mummery of devotion may still be performed with affected solicitude, but the moment that the æthereal fire of Christian love leaves the bosom, that moment every spark *of* VITAL *Christianity* expires. The fiends of darkness crowd into the heart which the spirit of Jesus has forsaken; and the pretended Christian ceases to have any more likeness to Christ, than the tyger, prowling in the desert, *has to the infant, smiling at the breast.*

A PICTURE OF
CHRISTIAN PHILOSOPHY.

Jesus on the cross, a martyr to truth.

Socrates died with dignity and composure, amid the soothing consolations, the flattery and the admiration of his friends. Jesus suffered a death more exquisitely painful; and the pain was encreased by every indignity which malice could contrive.

The firmness which is supported by applause, and by the expression of a cordial sympathy, sinks into dejection when attacked by scorn, humiliation and insult.

How beautiful is the prayer of Jesus! "Father, forgive them; for they know not what they do."—Since the time of Jesus, there have been several, who, inhaling his spirit of forgiveness, have at the very moment, in which they were undergoing the most excruciating sufferings implored, the divine mercy on their relentless persecutors. But does any part of history, anterior to the Christian æra, present us with an instance of the same kind?

The Indian, when tied to the stake, and put to a lingering death by the severest tortures, which are lengthened out, by ingenious cruelty, to their longest span of endurance, will bear pain with unshaken firmness. The early habit of supporting pain, assisted by certain ferocious sentiments of national glory, and of individual ambition, generates that hardiness which can stifle the exclamations of suffering; but he who seems fortified by insensibility against misery, rather excites the sublime sensations of wonder, than the tender ones of commiseration.—We cannot well sympathise with those sufferings which the sufferer does not feel. We often gaze on insensibility with aversion, but never with tenderness.

What, in the midst of his sufferings, are the ruling sensations of the savage? Are they those of benevolence and forgiveness? No;—they are the wild emotions of revenge, infuriated to madness.—Every accession of pain or aggravation of torture only incenses his vindictive rage. He utters the most bitter and unrelenting execrations against his persecutors; he calls on his friends and country-men to retaliate his injuries with ten-fold cruelty. His imagination anticipates the tortures of his oppressors; it pourtrays them in every writh and look of agony; and, so powerful is the energy of the vindictive principle, that the pleasures of revenge, though distant and uncertain, seem almost to absorb the pain of actual suffering.—In the hour of agony, the savage would revolt at the doctrine of forgiveness; his indignant spirit would spurn it as an inglorious act of pusillanimity or folly.

But lo! the difference between barbarous rage and Christian mildness. In the picture of Jesus, suffering on the cross, what a mixture is there of heroism with gentleness? How is his fortitude tempered by sensibility? He is not callous and impenetrable, but tremblingly alive to all the frail but truly captivating emotions of humanity. He does not affect a proud superiority to those feelings of pain, of which the privation or rather the insensibility is the result either of a brutal apathy or a disordered brain; and is never found in any character, that in the least deserves the name of amiable. The boasted indifference of the Stoic school is a point which mortality cannot reach; or which no one, who is acquainted with the pleasures and the consolations of sympathy, would wish to attain.

Sympathy is excited by a reciprocity of interests and of feelings; or, in other words, the interest which we take in the sufferings of others, is in proportion as we can identify their sensations with our own.—We can of course take no interest in the misery of one who is or seems to be insensate to the touch of pain. We can feel with those that feel, and who would accordingly sympathise with us in the like circumstances; but he, who is unconscious of his own sufferings, cannot be supposed to be easily affected by the sufferings of others. The power of sensation is associated with sympathy, and sympathy with the power of sensation.

The sufferings of Jesus excite a powerful interest; because he seems himself to have felt them with exquisite anguish. He was as feelingly conscious of his own miseries, as of those of others. When then we behold him stretched out in agony upon the cross, we cannot help melting into tenderness. Our hearts glow with the silent raptures of love and sympathy.—We hear rather with fondness than with aversion his plaintive and piercing cries in his last moments; we do not regard them as marks of imbecility; we cherish them as indications of humanity. They awaken emotions of tenderness, mingled with those of admiration; which are excited by the magnanimity of his forbearance, when we behold him disdaining the foul sentiment of vengeance and softening, in the midst of torture, to feelings of forgiveness. His benevolence is not altered by the tumult of barbarous outrage to which he was exposed; his meekness remains unchanged to the last; and he dies, as he had lived, in the divine and unblemished perfection of mildness and love.

The sufferings of Jesus are greatly ennobled by this consideration;—that they were a willing testimony to the truth. All truth, as well physical as moral is con-

nected with the well-being of man; but moral truth*
is of the greatest consequence, as it relates to the influ-

---

* A few men think for all the rest of the world. They give to opinions what shapes and complexions they think proper. The mere whistle of a name leads the mass of mankind astray, like a " will-with-a-wisp."
It was once the fashion to adopt no notions but those which had Aristotle's sanction. It is now a sort of high-treason to call in question certain tenets, on which certain great doctors, who have succeeded to the chair of presumption and infallibility, in which the Stagyrite used to sit, have affixed their seal of approbation.

The majority of minds are passive; they resemble wax which receives no impression, but that which is given to it by a power foreign to itself. —Whatever opinions some popular dogmatists may prescribe, they transfer, without hesitation, to their own stock; without staying to examine whether they be true or false, coherent or absurd.

Thus it happens, that by far the greater portion of what is called human knowledge, is nothing but an incongruous mixture of prejudices,—a crude consistence of truth, of error, and of folly.

Every opinion is a prejudice which is adopted without an enquiry into it's truth; and, if be on a perplexed and dubious subject, without at least balancing the probabilities that make for it's support or it's refutation. Opinions adopted from the mere " ipse dixit" of any authority, however great that authority may be, are equally prejudices with those which are adopted without enquiry.

However true the notions, in themselves, may be which we adopt without examination, they are no better than falsehood with respect to us, if not knowing the grounds on which they rest, we are neither able to justify them to ourselves nor to others.—To assent to any proposition, without knowing the arguments on which it is established, is a shameless contempt for the sacredness of truth. The first indication of a respect for truth is a repugnance to form hasty conclusions, or draw hasty inferences; but what can tend more strongly to season the mind with error, and to

ence of human conduct on human happiness; and is not merely related to a present and perishable, but to a

---

lessen the aversion to falshood, than the habit of concluding without evidence, and of inferring without knowing why?

The majority of people indeed are obliged rather to act than to think, and to employ the body more than the mind. But of those who have leisure for reflection, and whose aggregate numbers may be called the moral strength of nations, **how few are there who do not swallow opinions** like apothecaries **pills?—and they are** usually found to **turn to as little** nourishment.

But would men, instead of adopting opinions at random, seriously **examine their truth,** and particularly the truth of those which have a considerable influence on the happiness of mankind, would they but endeavour to analyse popular dogmas, instead of being enchanted by the witchcraft of great names, that veil of ignorance would soon be rent, which now hides some of the most beautiful parts of the shrine of truth.

The produce of truth must be in proportion **to the** number of minds **employed in** it's production. If, instead **of one person** thinking for **a thousand,** that thousand would venture to think for themselves, the progress of mind and the accumulation of knowledge would proceed with **a** thousand times it's present velocity.

There is no occasion to fear lest the means of supplying materials for the consumption **of** the aggregate energy of so many minds, should at last be exhausted. Truth admits not the relations of quantity. It is an infinite series; and is spread over an illimitable horizon.

The continually augmenting mental power of finite intelligences tends, by condensing particular into general truths, to approximate all the vari**eties of human knowledge** to unity; but without ever reaching it. The power of ultimate simplification belongs to God alone; to whom all time is as one instant present, all space **as one** point, and all the multifarious laws and complicated mechanism of universal nature as simple as a single **grain** of sand **upon** the shore.

future and eternal interest. It was for this truth, that Jesus suffered; and, in defence of which, he has taught us to make life a willing sacrifice.

The diffusion of truth can never be essentially injurious to mankind. For, though it may require the subversion of long-existed errors, and these errors, by mingling with it's benign, their malignant influence, may cause some disorders; yet it should always be remembered, that these disorders do not indicate the perniciousness of truth, but the obstinacy of error. All error being in itself an evil, the nature of counteracting causes will always occasion some evil to attend it's removal.

As any disease, long seated in the human frame, struggles against the remedies that are taken to remove it, and is not at last removed without much intermediate pain, so diseases in the body moral or politic seem, in some measure, to feel the energies of a self-preserving power; and are seldom effectually subdued without an obstinate resistance.

But we must be careful not to impute to truth the

mischiefs that belong to error; for it may be esteemed an incontestable maxim, that *truth is never mischievous.* It neither has nor can have any tendency to create disorder or to engender misery.—Truth is indeed the perfection of order, and the consummation of happiness; the highest attainment of reason, and the sublimest enjoyment of man.

There cannot be a more absurd or ruinous notion entertained than this,—That truth is occasionally pernicious. Truth and falshood are not of a changeable but a fixed nature. The first is essentially and radically good; the last is essentially and radically bad; independant of all local and temporal relations whatever. In the first therefore consists the happiness, in the last the misery of man; and no modification of circumstances ought, for a moment, to be permitted to set aside the sacredness of truth, or the ignominy of falshood.

If we were once to admit that any accidental relations whatever can alter the nature or deform the beauty of truth, we are guilty of denying it's fixed and unchangeable essence. Truth ought not to stoop to political or to individual convenience.—To pretend that what is truth to-day may be falshood and error in a change of circumstances, is to subvert, at one blow, all the relations that bind men together in society. We are changing a fixed and immoveable criterion of human actions, for one that is as precarious as the winds. Political convenience is shifting every hour; and if truth be to shift with it, and to follow it in all it's eccentricities, there is an end to it's existence. It is truth no longer; for truth implies immutability.

Political and private convenience ought to bend to truth; not truth to them; and of this be assured, O ye sons of Adam! that public happiness will rest upon a quicksand, till ye are universally convinced that ye can have *no interest distinct from truth*, and that it alone is the immortal basis of public and private glory!!!

Truth, being of a fixed unalterable nature, and as opposite to falshood as misery is to happiness, it ought not to be tampered with.

It ought not to be made the supple cameleon-like changeling of individual or political whim and artifice. Nor ought it *ever to be concealed*. To suppress the lively orracles or to veil the divine image of truth, in order to ferve any paltry ends of human policy, is to outrage the God of truth.

It was either a falfe delicacy or a defigning difhonefty which gave rife to this maxim:—" Truth ought not to be fpoken at all times. Moral truth,—that truth which is of an eternal and unperifhable influence, ought neither to be fhrouded in myftery or to be frittered away in ambiguity.—Truth, *the whole truth*, fhould be difplayed to the world, not tricked out with the harlotry of artifice; but beautiful in it's naked fimplicity. —The currency of gold may be affifted by a portion of alloy; but truth fhines brighteft when undebafed by error.

Were the nature and properties of truth juftly appreciated, and it's eternal value rightly underftood, there would be no occafion for any of it's champions to lay down their lives upon it's altar; but, at prefent, while error is fo much careffed, and falfhood fo ftoutly defended by corrupt and interefted hirelings, it is neceffary that the votaries of truth fhould be ready and willing to bleed in it's defence.

We should bear witness to the truth " looking unto Jefus," whose lips were never polluted with a falshood; and who taught his disciples that those shall gain life, who lay it down for his sake; or for the fixed, eternal and unchangeable truths which he promulgated; and which it is our duty to maintain, with unshaken courage, and at the expense of every worldly interest.

A PICTURE OF
CHRISTIAN PHILOSOPHY.

A future life—an immaterial principle—the truth of the resurrection of Jesus—practical inferences, &c. &c.

Few arguments for a future life are supplied by the view of nature. The world around us seems a perpetual struggle between life and death; a scene of incessant decay; a scheme of destruction always going on, and never completed.

The race of man appears as if born only to die. Successive generations successively disappear, and moulder into dust like their fathers. Virtue and vice, learning and ignorance obey the common sentence of mortality, and meet together in the grave.

What constitutes the spirit of man, or whether there be, in man, any spirit, distinct from his animal organization, the light of nature glimmering and dubious, cannot unfold to us. The human mind is often stored with many sublime ideas; it's conceptions soaring above worldly objects, at times, seem like the emanations of Pure Intelligence; yet there are some physical reasons for supposing that this very mind which seems impregnated, as it were, with fire from heaven, is no more than the result of the harmonious combination and vigorous exercise of material organs.* Our ideas are,

---

* We excel the brutes in no organ so much as that of touch; and which is the reason why our sensations are more exquisite than theirs. Perhaps men differ from each other in nothing more than in the greater or less excitability of their sense of touch; and, consequently, in the greater or less delicacy and distinctness of their sensations.

Perception is only a modification of sensation; and perceptions are strong and vivid, as sensations are distinct and lively. Thus the man of genius differs from others principally in the faculty of sensation.

Our senses of vision, hearing, smelling, tasting may probably consist in a greater excitability of the same power, which constitutes touch, residing in the eye, the ear, the palate, &c. &c. Thus in the olfactory nerves this power may be so exquisitely refined as to be excitable by invisible effluvia; in the nerves of the ear by the least vibrations of the air; in the nerves of sight by impressions as delicate and impalpable as the reflection of objects on the retina.

according to the opinions of the moſt acute philoſophers, the produce only of the ſenſes; and the ſenſes themſelves are evidently organic fibres, capable of excitement by their proper ſtimuli.

Our ſenſes are our only poſſible means of communication with the external world or with ourſelves. In other words, it is only through the medium of ſenſe, that we can obtain any knowledge of the world without us; and that we can attend to the reflex operations of our own minds. Take from man the ſenſe of feeling, hearing, taſting, ſmelling, ſeeing, he would be deſtitute of ideas, and incapable of reflection. It is, by means of our ſenſes, that we are able to retrace the ideas, with which they originally brought us acquainted, to diverſify their forms, and to arrange them under ſuch new

---

The ſuppoſiſtion, that all our ſenſes are only modifications of one and the ſame power (but which in particular organs, as the eye, the ear, the palate, is made ſuſceptible of different degrees of excitement) accounts for that parity and, as it were, unity of ſenſation, which conſtitutes, what may be called, ſelf-feeling.—Hence we can, at the ſame time, have the enjoyment of hearing, ſeeing, ſmelling, &c. without any confuſion or indiſtinctneſs of ſenſation; which would happen, if there were not ultimately and eſſentially unity in the ſenſorial power.

combinations, as that they sometimes appear to have no relation to any thing in nature, and to be the simple, spontaneous, unmixed progeny of the mind. But we can have no ideas that have not a sensual original.

It may be said, that our abstract ideas, as virtue, &c. which have no relation to sensible images, are attained, not through the medium of the senses of seeing, &c. but in some measure, by a total oblivion that we have such senses, or by a suspension of their operation. This error seems to spring from not considering, that all ideas, even those which are most complex, are nothing more than the combination of many particular ideas, and which are the offspring of individual and simple sensation.

In figures, we consider a collection of many particulars as constituting unity;—as, for instance, when we say a thousand, or a million. These are complex terms, of which, when we mention them in a rapid and cursory manner, we have no precise ideas, and can have none, till we resolve them into those simple and individual terms, of which they are abbreviations. It is the same in what are called abstract terms. When we mention the term, *virtue*, we have no fixed or definite ideas of the thing itself, till we come to consider it, as it were, under it's individual personalities, it's numerous subdivisions, and to sum up the particular terms, of which it is an abbreviation. Abstract terms ought to be always considered as abbreviations of many particulars; in the same manner as the term *a thousand* is of so many units. The necessity of these abbreviations arises from the limited capacity of the mind, which cannot attend to many particulars at once, and which, therefore, for the sake of expediting it's operations, that would otherwise be infinitely slow and tedious, has recurred to the invention of general and abstract terms.

As to abstract ideas, there are, in fact, no such things. An idea, means a distinct perception; and those persons, whose ideas are rather confused and fluttering vibrations, than distinct and definite perceptions, will find them but of little service, and producing ignorance rather than knowledge. Now when we mention any abstract idea, as virtue, what distinct perception have we of the thing itself? It is a word which we may easily pronounce; but of which, in fact, we can hardly have more definite notions than a parrot, till we have resolved it into it's several, simple, constituent ideas, and traced it through it's individual and particular relations. But having once done this, and having obtained, as it were, distinct perceptions of the meaning of the general term, we may, afterwards, apply it either in writing, or conversation, or reflection, with as much precision and advantage, as if all the particulars it includes were, at that very moment, present to the mind. *

---

* This shews the necessity of fixing a precise and definite signification to words; or otherwise, we must write and talk we know not what, like magpies and parrots. Some persons say, "if you have ideas you will never want words;" but the contrary rather holds good; for we can have but very few ideas without words; and as all our ideas, if we had no language, would be simple sensations, we could carry on no long train or process of reasoning, any more than we could count far without figures, or signs to express the different combinations of unity.

Those who can annex to each word they use it's definite and appropriate signification cannot be barren of ideas.

As the majority of our ideas have not a real, palpable and independant existence, their vitality, if I may so express it, consists merely in the symbols, which give them a "local habitation and a name." Those, therefore, who possess precise and definite notions of the meaning of these symbols, can hardly help being rich in ideas.

A mere vapid declaimer may indeed eructate all the froth of verbose oratory, though without accurately knowing, or rightly discriminating the terms he uses; but to use words with fitness, and so as to excite distinct perceptions, and to combine them with beauty so as to fill the mind, not with disproportioned and monstrous, but with natural and symmetrical images, shews a just taste and a well-regulated understanding.

If we have no ideas whatever that are not derived from the organs of sense, mere natural reason would, at first sight, lead us to conjecture that the mind perishes with the body. If the mind be a part, though the most perfect part of our animal organization, it seems necessarily involved in it's destruction.

But, perhaps, it will be said, that, though all our ideas are the product of the senses, there is in man a principle essentially different from the organs of sense; and that this principle is volition. †

The practice, therefore, of beginning education by teaching the precise signification of words is the best and most philosophic method. But, as words are the symbols of sensations, means should be taken, as much as possible, by means of diagrams and other contrivances, to excite the particular sensations they express. In other words—children should be made to acquire distinct perceptions of the terms they use. The progress of mind would then be greatly accelerated; the human understanding, no longer liable to be bewildered in the maze of crude half-formed notions, would not remain in a state of childhood, as it now often does, from infancy to old age.

† Volition, is that faculty which, according to the energy with which it operates in the individual, causes the intellectual faculties to act with greater or less vigor, and produces the various degrees of mental capacity.

But let us confider whether volition itfelf be a principle diftinct from our animal organization, or only a product of it.

The object of moft men, in every fphere of life, and in every direction, which the faculties take, is agreeable fenfation. This is the ultimate end of all the purfuits of man; and, in queft of this, he willingly incurs many difagreeable fenfations, which are often intermediate fteps to the object he defires. The defire of pleafure, though at a diftance, often overcomes the averfion to intermediate pain; and which may exceed the pleafure in reality, though not in the eftimation of the purfuer.

We are led, probably, by early fympathies, which give a peculiarly ftrong and lafting impulfe to individual defire, to affociate the idea of agreeable fenfation, in a more efpecial manner, with this or that particular purfuit. This caufes us to purfue it with eagernefs; it roufes the faculty of volition to endeavour, as it were, to feize it by great exertions.

It is a common and every-day expreffion, that men can do well what they have a genius for; which means no more than this;—that men can do well what they like to do well; or, in other words—that they ufually excel moft in that particular purfuit or employ, which fympathy or habit has made a fource of agreeable fenfation.

Agreeable fenfation is the ftrongeft ftimulus that can be ufed to excite volition; and the proficiency of men in any attainment, whether of art or fcience, is always in a direct proportion to the degree of voluntary power employed in it. "Poffunt quia poffe videntur." A ftrong degree of volition overpowers difficulties, which would appal the timid; and from which the luke-warm would fhrink with difmay.

Hence, Genius may be created. If you can once make a child firmly believe that his greateft happinefs refides in this or that particular purfuit; or, in other words, that fuch purfuit will be the means of a greater fum of agreeable fenfation than any other, it will become to him an object that will prompt to vehement defire, and to vigorous exertion. A thoufand

We are made by nature exquisitely sensible to pleasure and to pain. Hence we become acquainted both with **agreeable and** with disagreeable sensations; and **we can-**

---

associations, all flowing from, or connected with agreeable sensation, and directed towards the favourite object, will conspire to call forth more than ordinary energies of action.

Why do children usually love their play-things better than their books, but, because the former are to them a more prolific source of agreeable sensation? If **their books possessed a** greater power of agreeable sensation, they would throw away their play-things, as eagerly as they now usually lay aside their books. Hence, the motto for children's books ought to be, "delectare et prodesse;" and in the first period of childhood, at least, **no** books should be put into their hands which do not tend to improve them, by combining instruction with pleasurable sensation.

If you wish your child to excel in any particular pursuit, you must learn *artfully to manage the exciting power of sympathy*; you must endeavour, in very early life, to associate in his mind, with the object of excellence, every possible idea of agreeable sensation; which will act as a per**petual and** continually increasing stimulus, urging him to exert, in that pursuit with which he has been habitually used to connect sensations **of** pleasure, a peculiar and accumulated degree of voluntary power.

It is the strong and powerful excitement of volition, which counteracts **the "vis inertiæ,"** the gravitating force of sloth, that cramps even the moral powers of man; and which imparts to the natural sluggishness of the mind, the strength, the majesty and the swiftness of the eagle.

When a great degree of volition is excited, it always produces great exertions. Genius may be denominated, a high degree of volition employed in a particular **pursuit.** Hence the cause **of** the different modifications and kinds of genius.—Some connect the power of agreeable sensation either with poetry, or with oratory, or with any of the arts, more strongly than with any other pursuit. And hence, that particular pursuit becomes their predominant propensity. That is, always the predominant

not have been long in the world before the experience of the laſt has made us regret the abſence of the firſt.

---

propenſity of men, which, by having been, in their minds, moſt habitually aſſociated with agreeable ſenſations, has become, by the powerful but inviſible agency of ſympathy, the cauſe of their greateſt happineſs.

Why was Sir Joſhua Reynolds more fond of painting, than of ſtatuary, or of hunting, or fiſhing, or any thing elſe? Certainly, becauſe from ſome ſtrong ſympathy, excited in very early life, he had been led to aſſociate more agreeable ſenſations with the uſe of his pencil and his pallet, than with any other kinds of exertion. As he advanced in life, his fondneſs for his art, probably, increaſed. The pleaſures of imagination, unlike the groſs pleaſures of ſenſe, do not pall and grow faint, but increaſe and become more vigorous, according to the frequency of indulgence.

The agreeable ſenſations which Sir Joſhua had connected with his favourite purſuit, were augmented by many adventitious ſources of pleaſure,—by habit, by fame and by all the charms commonly aſſociated with celebrity. All theſe agreeable ſenſations were, in ſome meaſure, blended into unity; and produced an extraordinary degree of volition, which increaſed the power of excellence.

Men never purſue with that eagerneſs and ardor which is neceſſary to the attainment of excellence, or to ſplendor of ſucceſs, any thing which is not aſſociated in their minds with agreeable ſenſations, or with the idea of preſent or the hope of future happineſs.

Hence, genius often droops without a certain degree of encouragement; becauſe deſpair tends to baniſh agreeable ſenſation, which is the ſource of increaſed volition, and, conſequently, of increaſed activity of mind. On the other hand, great and extraordinary encouragement, or an unexpected acceſſion of wealth, or of the means by which a great ſource of enjoyment is at once put into our poſſeſſion, often tends, in the ſame degree, to produce languor, and relax exertion.

The **poſſeſſion** of great temporal advantages, increaſing the power of **gratification**, too uſually cauſes ſenſual to abſorb the deſire of mental plea-

From the sensations of pleasure or of pain, springs desire or aversion: and hence originates volition; which

---

sure; and, besides, we must consider that it is not so much the possession of pleasure, as the desire, combined with the hope of obtaining it, that stimulates to extraordinary activity.

That volition, which is the central **fire** of genius, is not so much kindled by objects, that are near and only a hand's-breath from us, as by those which are less distinct, and can only be seen, as it were, twinkling at the edge of the horizon.

Many a man of genius would have experienced a diminution of his energy, or an aversion rather than a desire to exert it, if he had enjoyed the full extent of those advantages, for which, perhaps, he anxiously sighed, and had been rewarded to the full boundary of his merit by pensions and emoluments.

Necessity, is the cradle in which genius is most frequently fondled to maturity. If the royal patronage did not impair the faculties of Johnson, **at least it** produced, except in one or two instances, a great unwillingness **to exert them.** His two great works, his Dictionary and his **Rambler,** of which the last will transmit his name to posterity, were produced in a state of indigence.

It would be a nice and most useful calculation, which should fix, **what degree of** encouragement ought to be afforded to men of genius, **and which would** rather invigorate than depress the active principle.

There have been, indeed, instances in which no encouragement, however great, and no neglect, however distressing, could, in the least, weaken the energies of the mind, or slacken the activity of pursuit. In these cases, an **impetuous** and overbearing desire of fame, rather than of the emoluments **of fortune,** has been associated with the object **of** pursuit, and rendered, by sympathy, the only source of agreeable sensation; and as this desire of fame can never be satisfied, but usually increases in proportion to it's gratification, it imparts to the volition an astonishing energy, and awakens all the powers of the soul to unwearied activity. It was this

is nothing more than the practical energy either of desire or of aversion. Volition, then, is the necessary result of the peculiar organization of our bodies. Possessing a frame so exquisitely adapted to the gentle or the violent impulses of pleasure or of pain, we, necessarily, will the one positively, and the other negatively.

Volition, is the ultimate result of sensation; and, accordingly, all animals * possess it, though in a far less degree than man, and proportioned to their degree of

---

love of fame which, in Milton, overcame obstacles that were almost insurmountable; and communicated to his genius a vigor more than mortal.

It is the passion for fame, that often renders the active principle capable of incredible exertions. Thus the truly-ambitious man,—he who feels in his bosom the ever-burning flame of that devouring passion, is commonly, in those pursuits in which his ambition centres, the most vigilant and indefatigable of men.

The reader will, I trust, pardon the length of this note, from it's relation to a subject of infinite importance to human happiness, I mean,—the *economy of mind*,—the most interesting topic in the whole sphere of human enquiry.—At some future period, I hope that I may have health and leisure to say more on this subject.

* The comparative feebleness of the voluntary power, in brutes, seems, to me, to be in a great measure owing to the greater comparative numbness, and, as it were, *locality* of their sense of touch,—that sense whose vitality and delicacy is present in almost every part of the human body.

irritability and sensibility. Natural reason, therefore, arguing from the nature of man, can by no means prove that volition is a principle distinct from the material tissue of the animal economy, or that it survives it's decay.

The voluntary power, whether it relates to the production of muscular or mental action, evidently sympathises with the declension of the power of animal life. As the fibres of our bodies, whether from the effects of intemperance, or sickness, or from the withering touches of age, become less irritable, volition grows more feeble.

Nothing can prove this more strongly than the decay of the memory* in drunkards and in old people; in whom, as the sensual fibres become less irritable to natural stimuli,

---

* Strength of memory, depends on strength of volition; and which again depends on the degree of sensation, by which it is excited. Thus we may account for the diversity of memories. All persons incline to remember, with most distinctness and accuracy, that which they have been most frequently used to associate, in their minds, with pleasurable sensations. These sensations invigorate the voluntary power; and which, in it's turn, impels and invigorates the power of **memory**.

and particularly to pleasurable sensation, the voluntary power becomes proportionally impaired. Memory is, indeed, only a modification of the voluntary power, reviving, according to the degree of it's energy, the past associations of the sensual fibres.

It has been said above, that the strength of volition depends greatly on the power of sensation; so it is remarkable, that old people can often more readily recal the events of their youth, than the transactions of yesterday; because the former have been more connected with agreeable sensations. These inspire the volition with an energy sufficient to revive the associations of youth; while it, in vain, strives to bring back more recent impressions. They elude the grasp of the will, and flit into eternal oblivion, like the dreams of the morning.

From what has been said on this subject, we must, I think, come to this conclusion—That our susceptibility of pleasure or pain, by exciting desire or aversion, necessarily creates volition. Volition, therefore, being in itself an effect, cannot survive it's cause; which, in an ultimate analysis, will be found to consist in the power of irritation and sensation; or, in other words, the vital principle (whatever it may be) which is inherent in all animal bodies, but more nicely modified in, and more exquisitely combined with those of the human species.

But it may be said, that we possess a principle of consciousness distinct from the principle of volition; and though connected with, by no means produced by, or resulting from our animal organization.

There seems a good deal of similitude between memory and consciousness;* but they are not essentially

---

* The author of Zoonomia says, vol. i. 132. "We are only conscious of our existence when we think about it; as we only perceive the lapse of time when we attend to it; when we are busied about other objects, neither the lapse of time nor the consciousness of our own existence can occupy our attention."

We appear never for a moment to be without the consciousness of personality; though *we do not always attend to it so far as to make it a subject of reflection.* All reflection is an exertion of volition, but not the smallest effort of volition is necessary to excite the idea of personality, unless when we desire to identify our present with our past being.—And I am inclined to believe, that the consciousness of personality is attached, though by an invisible and impalpable chain, to every one of our ideas; and is associated, even without our perceiving it, with every change that

the fame. Memory retraces the perceptions and relations of paſt time; but the power of conſciouſneſs concentrates our paſt ſenſations and perceptions in unity of time and place; and binds together the diverſity of our organic motions, in the perception of individuality or undivided perſonality. It is the power of conſciouſneſs which makes the preſent and the paſt contemporaneous, and incorporates all our notions and ſenſations in one ſimple notion and ſenſation of identity.*

There is a daily and hourly waſte of our frame.†

---

happens in the ſenſory. The contrary ſuppoſition would, at leaſt, corroborate that theory of ideas which was maintained by the acuteneſs of Berkeley and of Hume.

* May not *identity* have two ſignifications? one implying a ſenſation of our preſent individuality, the other connecting the idea of our preſent individuality with our paſt exiſtence?

† In the centre of every individual, there ſeems a conſuming power, which is continually oppoſing, and which finally deſtroys the power of life. Individuals ſoon periſh, if the daily aſſimilation do not balance the daily waſte. As the ſtrength of the ſtomach and inteſtines to aſſimilate the food we take to the animal matter of our bodies declines, the flame of animal life, wanting nutriment, grows fainter and fainter, till it is totally extinguiſhed.

An inceffant change is continually going on in us; and we never rife in the morning, with precifely the fame bodies in which we went to bed at night.

It is remarkable, that we fhould be confcious that we are the fame identic individuals now, that we were 12 or 20 years ago, when we, perhaps, retain not a fingle particle of the fame bodies we had then. The body keeps continually changing; but the confcioufnefs, as far as it refpects individuality, remains the fame and unchanged. Neither our paffions, our affections, our appetites, our defires, our averfions, our judgment, our volition, our memory, continue without change;—the confcioufnefs alone undergoes none.

Does there, not, therefore, feem to be, in every individual, a principle or power of confcioufnefs,[*] totally

---

In young, healthy and robuft individuals, the confuming power is confiderably lefs than the affimilating. In the meridian of life, the procefs of our deftruction and of our renovation, keeps pretty even; at a later feafon, if I may recur to a very common but apt illuftration, our fand runs out fafter than nature fupplies it, or than art can renew it;—and the worm finally feafts on our remains!!!

[*] The power of confcioufnefs, though it fhould not be immaterial, yet may be a fluid more fubtle than light or heat, fituated in the fenfory, and

distinct from the animal organization, and by no means dependant on it, or involved in it's diffolution? This confcioufnefs feems to be the fpiritual body which St. Paul mentions,* and which may be folded up in the natural; and which, after death, may grow and expand into a nobler exiftence; as the butterfly difplays it's variegated wings when the grub expires.

The natural world prefents but few arguments, or analogies, in fupport of a continuation of individual

---

fenfible to, but not itfelf altered by the elementary changes of the mortal body. It is no found objection to the exiftence of a power of confcioufnefs in the body, that it is not always perceptible, or that it cannot be brought within the cognizance of the fenfes. The fluid of gravitation is, probably, diffufed through every particle of matter, and yet we neither fee it nor feel it; nor have yet been able, by any palpable teft, to demonftrate it's exiftence. We have yet proceeded no farther towards proving it's exiftence, than can be done by alledging ftrong arguments againft it's non-exiftence.

It may be objected, that if we do poffefs fuch a principle of confcioufnefs, as I have ftated, diftinct from our animal nature, connected with it in life, but not affociated with it in death, why can we not connect, by the confcioufnefs of individuality, the earlieft period of infancy with our prefent exiftence? It may be anfwered, that the power of confcioufnefs, while it remains in the body, can exert no power independant of the organs, to which it is attached; but that when death has liberated it from the manacles of flefh, it will difplay it's energies pure and uncontrouled.

* 1 Cor. xv. 44.

existence; or in other words, of the extinction of consciousness in one state of being, and of it's renewal in another. In nature, we behold a most abundant provision made for the continuance of the species, but none for that of the individual. Every thing contains the principle of reproduction, either in itself, or by communion with it's kind. But if the progeny survive the death of the parent, they sooner or later mingle with the dust of their fathers.

Amid all the admirable contrivances of nature, for the reproduction of the species of all the myriads of organized nature, where shall we behold any for that of the same individual? Man himself seems to perish like the flower of the field. He lives, perhaps, a few years; he reproduces his kind; and he vanishes into darkness. The same individual is seen no more. He eludes our touch and our vision, like the shadow of the cloud that has passed over the earth.

The butterfly has, indeed, often been considered as a continuation of the individual, and an emblem of immortality. The grub, that disgusted by it's loathsome appearance, or that crawled on the earth in sluggish dulness, lies for a time in a state of apparent insensibility and death, till, at last, bursting it's coffin, it revisits the day-light, with gay and florid wings; delighting by the beauty of it's colours and the sprightliness of it's movements; and exciting sympathy in the beholder, by it's seeming consciousness of the agreeableness of it's own sensations. But is the butterfly at all conscious of having been a grub?

Where, and in what part of nature, will you find the most remote analogy of a continuation of individual consciousness? No where;—and without such a continuation, the individual is, in fact, annihilated, though the several parts of his former animal frame may pass into a thousand diverse forms, shapes and combinations. A continuation of the same individuality, means an annexed consciousness, connecting present and past identity. Without this, there can be no continuation of the same individual.

When the individual man dies, his body, resolving into it's primary particles, soon assimilates to the molecules of other bodies. But the individual suffers nothing by this process of deterioration, as long as none of his former confcioufnefs paffes into the vegetable or the worm. Again, fuppofe that the particles of the human body fhould, immediately after death, migrate into fome purer fubftance, which forms the nature of higher orders of intelligence. This ameliorated ftate of exiftence would, by no means, be a continuation of the fame individual, without an annexed confcioufnefs of paft identity.——But fuppofing, as feems probable, that there is a principle or power of confcioufnefs attached to every individual, diftinct from the animal economy, and not involved in it's diffolution, the idea of a future exiftence becomes more fimple and intelligible. The moment the individual perifhes, his confcioufnefs paffes into other regions, and allies itfelf to a more glorified body.

Some have confidered the general expectation of a future life, which feems to be diffufed over every region of the globe, and to have prevailed in all ages in the world,—as evidence of it's certainty.

The reftlefs longing after immortality, which feems a cheering fenfation, peculiar to the breaft of man, is by no means *a proof* that fuch a ftate awaits us. For we are fo organifed, and placed in fuch circumftances, that we could not well pass through life, without this sentiment being excited in us. Hence the untutored savage usually feels it, in as much, if not more vigor than the civilised philosopher.

Those who are conscious of a present existence, and can observe, as all but ideots must, and with some emotions of concern, observe the mortality of their fellow-creatures, cannot fail of contemplating their own mortality;—conscious that they now are, it is, at the very first view, revolting to the mind, to imagine a period when they shall not be. They are, therefore, naturally led, both by inclination and by hope, to contemplate death, not as an extinction of consciousness, but as a passage to another state of being.

The mind of every man, who can indulge the least thought on the subject, shrinks, with unspeakable horror, from the idea of annihilation,—an eternal extinction of present consciousness. This feeling, which Addison calls the " longing after immortality," if it be not innate, is, at least, a sensation that is always, sooner or later, excited by the mortality, to which we are subject, and of which we are often obliged to be the mournful spectators; and it seems a consoling ray, gleaming, though at an unmeasured distance, through the land of shadows.

Faint, however, and inconclusive are the best hopes of a future state, which are emitted from the light of reason. But, in proportion, as the intimations of such a state, from the analogies of nature, or the deductions of reason, are weak and unsatisfactory, so much the more probable is it, that the Almighty would vouchsafe to communicate to mankind such an important truth, by a particular revelation.

Such a revelation is, therefore, a priori, and reasoning on the attributes of benevolence, which we cannot help assigning to the Maker of all things, highly probable. And it is reasonable to suppose, that if the Almighty had not designed, from the beginning, such a revelation of a future state of being, he would have rendered the light of nature more conclusive on the subject.

When we sit down to examine the evidence of the resurrection of Jesus, with candour and seriousness, we can, by no means, dispute the possibility of it's truth, as some philosophers have done, a priori. For the fact must be rather confirmed than invalidated by such reasoning. Taking a comprehensive view of the moral world, we find that the credibility of an individual's rising from the dead, on purpose to convince mankind of a future state of existence, is, at first sight, confirmed by a thousand probabilities. But, when we come to find the fact itself supported by the most conclusive evidence—the evidence a " a priori," combined with a vast mass of "posteriori" evidence, amounts to a proof, little short of demonstrative, of the truth of the thing itself.

No "priori" evidence can, of itself, either prove or disprove the truth of any miracle; of which the reality must depend on the truth of the fact; and not on the presumptions which the wisest among beings, whose views are so limited as those of man, can form against it, from previous considerations on the general course or laws of nature.

We know but little of the general laws which regulate the course of the natural world; and we know still less of those moral laws which regard the conduct of intelligent beings, and the relations which may exist between them and the maker of all things.

Some individuals, intoxicated with the fumes of a false philosophy, will deny the *present* interference of God in the government of the world, and the welfare of mankind; but I do not see how we can allow that God made the world, without, at the same time, agreeing that he superintends it. Prescience does not exclude providence * A moral government is not incompatible with general laws; for if we allow that those laws were originally fixed by a moral governor, we must allow that they were, *from the beginning, adapted to moral purposes.* Those parts, therefore, in the moral system, which appear to us deviations from what we call the general laws of nature and ways of Providence, may be, in fact, only a part of them, though the sight is too dim to see their connection. These thoughts easily reconcile the notion of prescience, and of an over-ruling Pro-

---

* Prescience is here used as signifying fore-knowledge; Providence, as respecting the active presence of God, in the government of the world, disposing all things on the wisest plan, and making the different dispensations of good and evil subservient to purposes of benevolence.

vidence; for they are, in fact, the same thing; and the most subtle reasoners will find it difficult to prove the contrary.

The comets are, certainly, as regular in their apparently eccentric orbits and devious course, as the planets are in their more centrical rotations; but the regularity of the latter is more perceptible; and the regularity of the former would be equally so, if we were not quite so short-sighted, and could trace them more distinctly though the maze of their motions in illimitable space.

This may serve to illustrate the idea of the natural and moral order of the world. The former appears more regular and uniform, because it is placed, as it were, more in the region of our senses;—the last is equally regular; but as we are less acquainted with it's *whole sphere of action*, and can only observe a few of it's minute and detached parts, it appears, to our weak sight, a scene of chaos and confusion.

The Christian miracles, which are apparently irreconcileable with the general laws which prevail in the natural world, may be necessary links in the infinite chain of the moral system. They were ordained by prescience, from the beginning; and they were accomplished by providence, at the appointed time.

The assertion of Mr. Hume, that the Christian miracles must be necessarily false, because they are devious from the general laws of nature, is one of the most arrogant, not to say, impious assertions that was ever made. For Mr. Hume presumes to pronounce, on the universality of the laws of nature, to define the cases to which their application is limited, and the line beyond which they have no agency.

Vain man, whose whole existence is but a speck of time, canst thou measure the heights and depths of the divine prescience? Canst thou prescribe the barrier which infinite wisdom cannot pass?

The assertion of Mr. Hume, that it is more probable that testimony should be false than that miracles should be true, is a remark which is more specious than solid. For, in some cases, the knowledge of the human mind, of the natural affections and of the ordinary motives of human action will juſtify us in adopting the converſe of the propoſition.

In the caſe of the Chriſtian miracles, I think that a comprehenſive view of the principles of human nature will bear us out in the aſſertion, that it is more probable that the miracles themſelves ſhould be true, than that the teſtimony which was given in their defence, by the apoſtles and firſt Chriſtians, ſhould be falſe.

Omitting the conſideration of the other Chriſtian miracles, I ſhall wholly confine myſelf to that particular miracle of the reſurrection of Jeſus, on which the truth of Chriſtianity reſts, as on a baſe of adamant.

In combating the great authority of Mr. Hume, I ſhall begin with ſtating this propoſition,—that " the reſurrection of Jeſus is more likely to have been true, than the teſtimony which maintained it to have been falſe;" and this I hope to prove, to the ſatisfaction of the reader.

The fact itſelf, as I have before remarked, is rather confirmed that invalidated by conſiderations " a priori."

It is a fact, entirely consonant to the best notions, which the most enlarged reason can form of the divine wisdom and goodness. It is a fact, which it was worthy the supreme disposer to establish, in order to determine the inconclusive reasonings, and to fix the wavering hopes of man about a future state. It is a fact, which, if it seem derogatory to the natural order of events, and to the general course of nature, was yet essentially requisite to harmonise the chaotic confusion that otherwise prevails in the moral world.

If God be a moral governor, we must suppose that he has placed eternal and immutable distinctions between virtue and vice, cruelty and benevolence; but as we do not observe such distinctions here, as we do not behold happiness invariably associated with virtue, or misery with vice, we thence infer the probability that the Almighty would vouchsafe to his creatures some consolatory intelligence of another life after death, in which the irregularities of the present scheme of things will be corrected.

The knowledge of a future life is likewise absolutely necessary to fix moral truth on a strong foundation;

and to strengthen moral obligations, by an eternal necessity and importance. For, supposing there to be no future life, morality has no other sanctions than what temporary expedients, or than what the convenience or the caprice of individuals may bestow. Men are let loose at once, from all restraints, but those few which civil society imposes, and which can never reach that depravity which lurks in the hidden chambers of the heart. It is nothing but the conviction of a future life, and of a day of recompence after death, which *can operate to the prevention of secret crimes;*—crimes which may be committed with civil impunity, and without any dread of temporal shame.—It is this conviction alone which can purify the bosom from a base and narrow selfishness, and open the heart to the pleasures of a disinterested benevolence.

Where men have not the least hope or expectation of a life after death, self, and self only will be their idol; they will not heed those moral relations, in the midst of which, man is placed; and for the contempt of which he is accountable. They will scoff at those benevolent sympathies which tend to approximate the interest of individuals to those of their fellow-creatures.

He who looks to the grave, as the scene of endless annihilation, as the last limits of human destiny, will necessarily feel a cold aversion to every generous act of self-denial, and to every great exertion in the cause of suffering humanity. Far different will it be with him, who, beholding the glorious light of eternity, shining beyond the "valley of the shadow death," connects the influence of his present conduct with his future condition; and associates an immortal interest with a scrupulous regard to the observance of justice, and the practice of benevolence.

Of such importance is the belief of a continuation of existence beyond the grave! Some satisfactory information, on a subject of such infinite concern, it was certainly worthy the Governor of the world to communicate; and it is so far probable, from previous considerations, that the case of the resurrection of Jesus, to which Christians appeal, as the medium of this communication, is not a vain fable but a certain fact.

It now remains for us to consider, whether the resurrection of Jesus be supported by probable and competent testimony.

In the first place, it is more natural and easy, from the influence of the principle of association, to speak truth * than falshood; and, perhaps, in the most profli-

---

* Children possess naturally a love for truth and an aversion to falshood. Were the first universally and judiciously encouraged, it would never be vanquished by the second; which, by bad management, is often changed from an aversion into an affection.

When parents punish their children for telling the truth, they cause them, in future, to take an interest in falshood. Their natural antipathy to the latter vanishes; and, as they grow up, they learn to associate it with the pleasures of self-interest. Parents cannot too soon instil into their children this sound maxim of true philosophy and genuine Christianity,—that there is an intimate connection between falshood and misery.

If, on any occasion, you punish your child, when he ingenuously confesses the truth, you will, afterwards, cause him to hesitate about confessing it; till, at last, perhaps, he will flatly deny it, or boldly persist in a false assertion.

How soon does a passion for discovering the true relations of things, which is, in fact, no other than a passion for truth, disclose itself in children! What is called infantine curiosity, is a species of this passion. It originates from a desire to behold things in their just and real, not their seeming, relations; and is mingled with an aversion to be misled by appearances.

You, perhaps, give your child a watch, or some other toy; and you almost immediately find a desire excited to behold the inside and to discover the true relation between that and the outside appearance.

The principle of the love of truth in children is seen even in their credulity. Conscious of their own sincerity, they are but too apt to think others equally sincere, till sad experience teaches them that fraud and dissimulation are the too prevailing characteristics of mankind!!!

gate liars, the number of their affirmations which are true, or which they conscientiously believe so, greatly exceeds those which are false, or which they wilfully pronounce with a consciousness of their untruth.

Truth to be spoken, and to be spoken with consistency, requires no pains; but falshood, by counteracting the natural sentiments, and by being counteracted by those numerous associations of ideas, which serve as preservatives to veracity, cannot be maintained, with any steadiness, without *extraordinary exertions*.

Men are never impostors and liars *without a motive*; and, as there always is, in every individual, from causes which attach to his organization, a desire to speak the truth, *that motive* must be stronger than the biafs of nature and association, which inclines him to truth and sincerity. *

---

* The doctrine of counteracting motives, has never yet been sufficiently considered or elucidated. Could we ascertain the force of oppofing motives, which are, as oppofing powers at the two ends of a beam, with an accuracy approaching to algebraic precifion, we might then reduce the competency or incompetency, the truth or falshood of testimony to mathematical certainty.

The primary and most important question, which arises in considering the truth of the resurrection of Jesus, is this; supposing the fact a scandalous imposture, what motive could the apostles have had, sufficient to counteract their natural love of truth, and to make them attempt to palm upon the world an unfounded falshood?

Happiness or agreeable sensation, either in possession or reversion, is the common incitement to human action. Now, what interest could the apostles have had, in this assertion, that "Jesus was risen from the grave?"—an assertion which involved them in an unexampled series of persecutions and sufferings?

In the time of the Apostles, the love of life was as strong a principle of action as it is at present. The love of life is perhaps the strongest principle in our nature. It is that which commences with the first beat of the heart and continues to it's last. Associated with the love of life is the desire of enjoying it, or, in other words, of agreeable sensation. The combination of these two powers energises the principle of self-interest.

This principle of self-interest is never totally extinguished in the human breast. It is often, as it were, dormant; but is never dead. It is a fire, which is sometime seen beaming benignly, at others burning destructively; and fuel is never wanting in the heart to keep it in a state either of slow and gentle, or of furious and violent combustion.

It is to the principle of self-interest, that the motives of human action may always be traced; though, in some actions, we are obliged to ascend to the parent source by a much more circuitous rout than in others. Self-interest is a fountain, from which flow a variety of streams, meandering in a thousand directions.—Thus, self-interest operates differently in different individuals; some pursue a real and palpable, others a propable and apparent interest; some a present, others a future and distant interest.

The great difference, therefore, between good and bad men is, that the latter act solely with a view to a present, the former more with a view to a future interest and reward. While the one pursues happiness through the medium of sensuality, the other pursues it through

P

the medium of benevolence, or of agreeable sensation, moral and refined.

That the Apostles had no *present interest* in view when they affirmed, at the hazard of life and all it's enjoyments, that Jesus was risen from the dead, cannot be denied. Their motives must, therefore, be referred to a future interest,—an interest which they were not to taste till after death. Now the only probable ground on which this expectation could be raised, was the conviction of this truth, that Jesus was risen from the dead; and this conviction must have been strong and well-grounded indeed, when it could enable them to subdue those propensities of sense, which urge men to worldly pleasures; and when it could cause the hope of a future and invisible joy to absorb the energetic passion of the love of life, which so wonderfully strengthens the power of a present self-interest.

Were the Apostles and first Christians so totally different in their nature from other men, that they acted not from the love of pleasure but of pain, not of happiness but of misery? Did they seek these things for their own sakes?—for allowing the resurrection to have been their own fiction, we can affign no other motives whatever to their conduct; but if we allow the fact, we fhall then find an eafy and fimple folution of their behaviour; and it admits of an explanation from the known principles of human nature,—*principles, from which man never deviates, any more than the planets from their orbits.* The Apoftles did not purfue pain and fuffering for their own fakes; agreeable fenfation was as much the object of their exertions as it is of human activity in general; but, in order to obtain it, they voluntarily encountered a long and dreary ftate *of intermediate affliction.* They clearly faw that much prefent mifery lay before them, but that glory and immortality awaited them, at the end of their labours. Their conduct, therefore, was regulated more by a future than a prefent felf-intereft; by agreeable fenfation after death rather than before it.

Allowing the conduct of the Apoftles and firft Chriftians to have been fuch, as facred and profane hiftory concur to reprefent it,—and, moreover, allowing the general principles and ruling motives of human action to have been the fame then, that they are at prefent,— the truth of the refurrection of Jefus becomes eftablifhed

P 2

by proofs which do not come far fhort of demonftrative certainty.

The degree of affent which we give to teftimony ought, certainly, to be proportioned to the credibility of the witneffes, and to their compatibility. The credit due to the witneffes for any fact is according to their character for veracity, and to the means they had of knowing the truths they affert. I do not fee how the credibility of the witneffes of the refurrection can be impeached, either by their want of integrity, or common fenfe, or competent information.

In afferting fuch a fact, they could not, as we have feen, have been biaffed by any bafe motives of felf-intereft; for felf-intereft inclined the other way; and we cannot, for a moment, imagine that they themfelves were deceived, or that their fenfes were impofed on.

The death of Jefus, on the crofs, was a fubject of public notoriety. Of this the Apoftles had palpable demonftration; and they had proof, equally demonftrative, of his refurrection. And they were not difpofed to assent to such a fact, without such evidence as was fully satisfactory, and which could not be disputed.

Credulity, which has rendered so many the dupes of imposture, was far from being a trait in the characters of the Apostles. Instead of inclining to a faculty of of belief, *they were rather disposed to indulge doubts and to entertain cavils.* The most astonishing miracles could *hardly conquer their unbelief.* " O fools," said Jesus, " and slow of heart to believe !" Luke xxiv. 25.

Though Jesus had repeatedly declared to his disciples, that he should rise again from the grave,* yet these declarations made but little impression on them. After his crucifixion, they seem to have mourned and wept, as for one whom they should see no more ! Mark xvi. 10. And even after that they had been told, by Mary Magdalene, that Jesus was risen; St. Mark informs us, that *they believed not;* and St. Luke xxiv. 11. says, that *her words seemed to them as idle tales.*

---

* Vid. Matt. xx. 19. xxvi. 32.

Thus we see that the Apostles were, by no means, disposed to believe, that Jesus was risen from the grave, *without sufficient evidence*. They were too incredulous to have been made the dupes of imposture, even if any had been attempted. But Jesus gave the Apostles the most convincing proofs that his resurrection was neither a deceitful fabrication nor an ideal supposition—" Behold," said he to them, Luke xxiv. " my hands and my feet, that it is I, myself; handle me and see me." He did not appear to them in a vision of the night, when the vigilant and scrutinising powers of man are suspended; and the imagination, liberated from all restraint, is abandoned to the illusions of an ideal world. He did not appear *to one individual only*, in a state of solitude; when his terrors might have overpowered his judgment. But he appeared to the eleven disciples, as they were assembled together; and offered himself to be handled and seen; that they might be assured, that he was not a mere phantom, conjured up by their own imagination. On this occasion, St. Luke xxiv. 41. tells us, that at first " *they believed not for joy.*" How natural and how lively is this representation of the Evangelists! The events which we ardently desire, and yet but little expect we can hardly bring ourselves to believe, when they come to pafs. The fulnefs of our joy almoſt inclines us to doubt our own fenfes, and to diftruſt the reality of our good fortune.

That the impreffion, made on the minds of the Apoſtles, might not be obliterated, and that every doubt which they could poffibly entertain of the truth of his refurrection might be diffipated, Jefus appeared to them at *several* other times;—once when he convinced Thomas, who was not prefent at his firſt appearance, John xx. again, John xxi. he ſhewed himſelf to the difciples, at the fea of Tiberias; when he converfed and eat and drank with them; and again, in Bethany, when he afcended into heaven, in the prefence of five hundred of the brethren; of whom many were living when St. Paul wrote his Firſt Epiſtle to the Corinthians.

Thus we fee that the refurrection of Jefus was confirmed by indifputable teſtimony, by witneffes, *not in the leaſt credulous or biaſſed, and who refuſed to admit it's truth till they could no longer doubt it.*

The bold and *difintereſted* declarations of the truth of the refurrection, which the Apoſtles made in the prefence of those by whom Jesus had been crucified, and soon after that event, deserve particular attention.

St. Peter, in a speech which he delivered on the day of Pentecost, Acts ii. resolutely and undoubtingly affirms the truth of the resurrection; and this he does, in defiance of that infamous lie, which the Jewish rulers had propagated, That the disciples had stolen the body. The Apostle then tells them, " That God had raised up that Jesus whom they, by wicked hands, had crucified and slain." Observe what a solemn conviction of this important truth, must have influenced the Apostle at this moment, and how fearless this conviction made him! For, *the mere assertion of the fact, at such a time*, was a charge of atrocious murder and of shameless falsehood, against the whole Jewish government; who had first put Jesus to death, and then fabricated a lie, to conceal the truth of his resurrection. Was it probable, then, that any one of the Apostles * would thus have

---

* Consider the pusillanimity of the Apostles, *before the resurrection* (when they *all forsook their master*, and one positively denied him), and compare it with their open avowal of him, *after his resurrection*,—an avowal which no menace nor persecution could, *for a moment*, induce them to retract.

dared to criminate those, who had so lately nailed their master to the cross, if they had not been assured, by irrefragable proofs, that Jesus had triumphed over the grave, and that opened to them a way from temporal pains to immortal happiness?—When the Apostles had miraculously healed a man, who had been a cripple from his birth, St. Peter told the admiring Jews, that they had not performed this cure through their own power, or holiness; but " through faith in the name of the Prince of life, whom God had raised up, of which they were witnesses." Acts iii. 15.—In the ivth of Acts, we read, that the Apostles were apprehended for having preached, through Jesus, the resurrection from the dead: being carried before the great council, they were required to tell, by what means they had made the impotent man whole. Not in the least dismayed, they boldly declared, " Be it known unto you all, and to all the people of Israel, that by the name of Jesus Christ, whom ye crucified, whom God raised from the dead, even by him doth this man stand before you whole. Neither is there salvation in any other," &c. This is the undaunted language of conscious truth. When the Apostles were dismissed from the council, they were peremptorily ordered, neither to preach nor teach any more in the name of Jesus. But Peter and John, unmoved by the menace, answered, that " they could not but speak the things *which they had seen and heard.*

Another illustrious witness of the resurrection is St. Paul. To suppose that St. Paul, a man of strong natural sagacity, versed in all the learning of the Jews, animated with the zeal of the Pharisees, and burning with rage against the Christians, should, *in a moment*, and *without any cause adequate to a divine influence*, become the strenuous and indefatigable advocate of that religion which he had so bitterly persecuted;—to suppose that he should, *in an instant*, renounce all those notions in which he had been brought up, and the prejudices of the sect, to which he had been so warmly attached, is utterly incredible, and contrary to the well-known principles of human nature, and motives of human conduct. His sudden and extraordinary conversion, can only be accounted for by allowing the truth of that miraculous interposition of divine power, which is recorded by St. Luke, and which is corroborated by the voluntary testimony of St. Paul himself. The Apostle of the Gentiles was convinced that the tale of the Jewish rulers was an artful endeavour, to suppress the glorious truth of the resurrection; for he saw and conversed with that Jesus whom they had crucified.

But it may be said, that, allowing the Apostles to have been, in every respect, credible and competent witnesses; we cannot be assured that their testimony, as recorded in the Gospels and Acts, &c. is that which they delivered to the world. It may be alledged that the validity of testimony decreases, in proportion to the distance from the time when it was first delivered, or that the probability of it's truth is inversely as it's distance. This objection, though it possesses some weight, yet will be found not to have much, in the case of that testimony, which the Apostles and first Christians gave to the truth of the resurrection.

The authority of testimony is, by no means, diminished by the lapse of time, unless it can be proved, that it has been either mutilated or corrupted in it's descent. If this cannot be proved, it's authority remains, at the end of a thousand years, as strong, and essentially as convincing as it was at the beginning.

When we consider, therefore, the evidence, by which

the truth of the resurrection is established, we ought to inquire whether there be any proof of it's having been altered in it's descent from it's original source?

Of the writers, whose written testimony, in favour of the resurrection, has come down to us, we have not the least grounds for presuming that the relation has experienced any material changes or depredation, in it's transmission through so many centuries.

The sacred books were preserved with scrupulous fidelity; and the dissentions, that begun to prevail in the Christian church, even in the age of the Apostles, greatly contributed to maintain the purity and integrity of the text, in all points of consequence. Had the Christian church continued, from it's first beginning to the present time, undisturbed by the jealousies of schism, or the commotions of faction, the charge, That the text of the sacred books had been, at different periods, mutilated and perverted, to suit the interested views of priestly artifice, might have been urged by the skeptic with more force and plausibility; and could not so readily have been refuted. But, *fortunately*, Divine Providence so ordered it, *that differences of opinion should prevail in the church from it's earliest periods;* and these differences have not only prevented the religious principle from sinking into a fatal languor, but have eminently contributed to preserve, pure and inviolate from profane hands, the text of the sacred writers. For, had one party attempted to alter the books of the Evangelists, to suit their private views, and to give a preponderance of authority to their favourite opinions, their attempts would instantly have been exposed by the adverse faction; the cry of sacrilege would have been raised, which would have brought shame and derision on those, whose audacity had perpetrated such an outrage on the holy volume.

In the various dissentions, about forms of faith and points of doctrine, which have taken place in the Christian church, and which certainly have not been characterised by liberality, or softened by mildness, all parties *appealed to the same authority,*—the records of the Apostles and Evangelists; and seem to have combined, notwithstanding their mutual animosities, to preserve them pure and incorrupt.

When the dissentions of the Christian church had

settled into that dead and fatal calm, which, under the benumbing influence of an intolerant superstition, overspread the Western hemisphere, then, indeed, a fair opportunity presented itself, to mar the sacred text, to suit the purposes of priestcraft; and to glut the rapacity of Papal ambition.

But no such attempt was made; and if it had been made, it must have miscarried; first, from the ignorance, which prevailed among the clergy, of the original language in which the gospels were written; and, next, because, if the manuscripts of the Western church had been surreptitiously mutilated and interpolated, the genuine text would still have survived in those of the Eastern or Greek church.

That no corruptions have found their way into the New Testament, which can, in the least, shake the fundamental stability of the Christian religion, we may learn from this, that, of all the various readings,* which

---

* The various readings, in Mills's edition of the New Testament, have been computed to amount to thirty thousand.

the diligence of critics has hitherto discovered, there are none which, in the least, tend to invalidate the truth of any fact of importance. Amid an almost incredible multitude of minute and unimportant variations, all the manuscripts of the Evangelists which have hitherto been collated, *harmonize in recording the facts, which are most material to the cause of revelation.* There are verbal differences; there are omissions, and there are corruptions of little moment; but when we give to these, their individual and their collective weight; they will be found rather to add to, than to deduct from the consistency and the authority of the Evangelical testimony.

That the Evangelic records themselves were written in the age to which they are ascribed, is sufficiently clear from contemporary history; and it is equally clear, that the validity of their attestation to the truth of the miracles and of the resurrection of Jesus, remains the same, at this day, as it was on their first publication to the world. Distance of time has not therefore by any means impaired the consentient force of the apostolic testimony to the truth of the resurrection of Jesus from the dead; because the testimony, in favour of this fact, which was given immediately after the event, has remained unchanged ever since.

But Mr. Hume would say, that allowing in all it's extent the sincerity and the credibility of the testimony, still, that the resurrection of a dead man to life, being contrary to the general laws of nature, and to all the accumulated observations of the great mass of mankind on the operations of those laws, must be necessarily false, and what no testimony can prove true. But I must observe, that we know little of the generality or permanency of the laws of nature themselves, but from the testimony of past generations. When we predicate their universality, *we, in fact assume the truth of testimony*.

It is from testimony only, that we know that there has been, for the last two or three thousand years, a regular succession of seasons, or that the sea has experienced a flux and reflux, or that the air has been disturbed by tempests, or that the moon has, at certain regular periods, waned and increased, appeared and disappeared.

These are laws of nature; but, of their universality,

of the regularity and, as it were, continuity of their operations, in time paſt, we really know no more, than thoſe have told us who have gone before us; and whom we may number back for many ages, till we arrive at the confines of an impenetrable obſcurity. Did we not give ſome credit to teſtimony, we ſhould, at laſt, believe nothing but what came within the cognizance of our ſenſes.

It is only from teſtimony, we know that this earth has been inhabited, by man, for five or ſix thouſand years. It is only from teſtimony, we know that this world has, during that period, been cheered by the influence of the ſun, or that the heavens have been illumined with ſtars.

The philoſopher may ſay, that, obſerving with his own eyes the great regularity which, at preſent, exiſts in the motions of the heavenly bodies, and the great uniformity which is viſible, in what are called the laws of nature, he is convinced that their regularity and uniformity have always been the ſame. But whence can the philoſopher, who will give no credit to teſtimony, believe, that with which none of his ſenſes have made him acquainted;

and for which he can bring no other proof, than the proof of testimony; to which, he pretends that he ought not to assent? His belief of the universality and uniformity of the laws of nature, must depend on the credit which he gives to the testimony of others, confirmed by the researches of his own reason into the natural order of things, at present existing in the world.

Now, does Christianity demand belief on less substantial grounds? No;—it requires nothing more than an assent to the truth of the testimony,—not against reason;—but on rational principles, and from serious enquiry. Christianity, by no means, requires an acquiescence in the truth of the testimony, by which it is established, without *a previous examination* into it's validity and it's credibility. It calls for such examination first, and for such acquiescence afterwards: and I feel a firm persuasion, that if the most acute philosophers would but investigate the truths of Christianity, with that seriousness and candour, which they themselves would be the first to recommend in other subjects of investigation, that they would be as strongly convinced that Jesus rose from the dead, as they are that the earth has experienced, for the last two thousand years, regular vicissitudes of summer and winter, or that the moon has been subject to periodical revolutions. The philosopher may say, that he does not disbelieve such things, because he observes the course of nature to be the same at present, and that, therefore, in these cases, his assent to past testimony is confirmed by present observation;—but, that when testimony requires him to assent to the truth of a dead man's having risen again to life, he cannot subscribe to it, because it is contrary to present experience; and because all the observations which he can make on the irresistible mortality of the human species, and on the immutability of the laws of nature, contradict it's probability; and are arguments against it's truth, which no testimony can establish.

It must be allowed, nevertheless, that we know nothing of the identity between the present and the former course of nature but from the truth of testimony. It is from testimony we learn that there was, in former ages, the same regularity and uniformity in the natural world, and the same instability, and, as it were, fragility in the moral, that there is at present.

The most skeptical must allow, that, at least, a considerable part of human knowledge is founded on human testimony. And though there may, in particular parts of such knowledge, as is derived from testimony, be an intermixture of falshood, still *the great mass of it is truth.*

From the influence of association, and from the greater natural facility of speaking truth than fashood, truth acquires a power over the heart that may easily be diminished, but is seldom, if ever, entirely extinguished.

Hence, the combinations of falshood are usually the means of their own detection. Such is the secret and invisible power of truth, that it is difficult indeed for any individual to be consistent in a lie;—I mean such a lie as involves a multiplicity of events, an intricate detail of great and minute circumstances;—but for many individuals to persevere in such a fabrication, without such glaring incoherencies and inconsistencies, as should be their own refutal, is next to impossible.

Falshood, by being always associated, at least, with some degree of aversion, requires a greater effort of the mind than truth; the latter, according with the natural feelings of rectitude, and connected with agreeable senfation, flows, as it were, from the heart with eafe and promptitude; while the former counteracted, in almoft every ftep of it's progrefs, by the natural fentiments, the affections and the affociations of the mind has to encounter obftacles, that are not readily fubdued. Thus we fee that nature has provided for the defence of truth, and particularly the truth of teftimony, by oppofing fo many difficulties to confiftency in falfhood.

Carrying the foregoing obfervations in his mind, let the moft fkeptical fit down to examine, with ferioufnefs and candour, the truth of that teftimony, by which the fact of the refurrection of Jefus from the dead is fubftantiated. Let him carefully weigh the nature of the teftimony, it's multiplicity, it's variety, it's confiftency; and then let him compare it with the circumftances of the witneffes.

Let the fkeptic confider, amid a multitude of minute and unimportant variations, and which are rather a proof of undefigning integrity, than of defigning forgery, what a perfect confiftency and harmony there is in the whole mass of the testimony, and what an air of candour, of truth and simplicity pervades the whole narrative of the fact, in the Four Evangelists. There are no marks of that disguise, that duplicity, that embarrassment, which are almost necessarily attached to falsehood. The relations of the Evangelists possess those inimitable features of an easy, unassuming confidence, which are characteristic of artless veracity.

The skeptic should, likewise, contrast the circumstances of the witnesses with the testimony they delivered. Did their testimony tend to improve their circumstances? Certainly not. It involved them in indigence and misery; but this indigence and misery they voluntarily endured, *rather than keep back the testimony.*

Men never act without motives. The motive that could urge the Apostles to persist in such a gross and palpable falsehood, as the resurrection of Jesus to life (supposing it to be a lie of their own invention), must have been strong indeed, to overcome their natural love of truth, and to sear their hearts against those sensations of remorse and shame, which, at least, in some degree, are the invariable associates of imposition and of falshood.

But, in the case we are considering, what motive could there have been powerful enough to operate this effect? The prospect of some great temporal advantage has often induced men to maintain, with resolute effrontery, and, at every hazard, some artful scheme of interested imposture; but there never yet was an instance, in which men have persevered in such a scheme, for the sake of pure, unalloyed and hopeless misery. And yet we place the Apostles in these very circumstances; we make misery inconsolable, and wretchedness unqualified, the object of their wishes, and the end of their exertions, if we suppose the resurrection of Jesus to be nothing more than a cunningly devised fable, of their own invention.

Supposing the truth of Christianity a fiction, it is absolutely impossible, that the conduct of the Apostles should have been such as sacred and profane history concur to represent it; and as the circumstances of the world, at that time, combine to prove that it must have been. It is full as improbable, that twelve men, in their senses, should perſiſt in a lie, for the ſole ſake of exchanging comfort for anguiſh, and happineſs for miſery, as that a dead man ſhould riſe to life. The former is as great a deviation from thoſe moral laws, which influence the courſe of human actions, as the latter is from thoſe natural laws, which cauſe the mortality of the human ſpecies.

If the philoſopher will not allow the truth of one miracle, he muſt, at leaſt, allow the truth of what is quite as miraculous, full as improbable, and quite as irreconcileable to the ordinary courſe of events.

The conduct of the Apoſtles, not to mention others, who were all men of ſound judgment, good common-ſenſe, and plain, unſophiſticated underſtandings, cannot poſſibly be reconciled to any experience of human nature, or to any knowledge of human motives,— without allowing the truth of the Chriſtian miracles, and particularly that fundamental miracle, the adamantine baſe of the Chriſtian doctrine,— the reſurrection of Jeſus from the dead.

Can any philoſopher allow that the general principles of human nature, and the general incitements to human action, were the same in the days of the Apostles, that they are at present, without allowing the sincerity and integrity of their testimony, and the consequent truth of the facts which it records? Can any philosopher, who is capable of calm and dispassionate reflection, for a moment imagine that so many individuals, all capable of feeling pain and pleasure, and distinguishing their differences, should, without a single interested motive, either of pleasure, fame or fortune, voluntarily engage in a long and heart-rending scene of complicated agonies, for no other purpose, than to vindicate assertions which they knew to be false?

In every view, which I can take of the subject, it appears to me that the converse of Mr. Hume's proposition, is that, which in this instance, we ought to embrace; and that "it is far more probable that the resurrection of Jesus should be true, than that the accumulated testimony in it's favour should be false."—The Philosopher, who obstinately perseveres in denying a miracle, which is so well attested, only because it appears to his dim perceptions and limited capacity, contrary to the usual course of nature, seems, in some degree, to resemble a person, who should refuse to believe, that other countries were subject to the concussion of earthquakes and the desolation of volcanos, because he had never observed them in his own; and therefore might suppose such phenomena, contrary to what his narrow observation might induce him to think the ordinary course of nature.

The obstinate aversion to believe in a miracle, so well attested as that of Christ's resurrection, would vanish, if the unbeliever would consider—that the world has moral as well as natural laws, and, that the resurrection of a dead man to life, though it may seem contrary to the latter, might, in the particular instance which is alledged, have been highly agreeable to the former; and he should besides consider—that a serious and comprehensive enquiry into the system of nature and the ways of providence, would prove natural and moral laws to be essentially the same, and to harmonize exactly in all their operations; and that the resurrection of Jesus from the dead, though apparently anomalous to the first, might, at the time, and in the circumstances, in which it took place, have been analogous to both.

Allowing the truth of the resurrection of Jesus, the practical inferences, that are to be derived from it, must be obvious to every one.——The question about the nature of the sentient principle, whether it be formed of perishable or imperishable materials, whether it be a combination of grofs matter, or a spark of æthereal fire, whether it survive the body or mingle with it's dust, is of little importance; when we know that " Christ is risen from the dead, and become the first fruits of them that slept. For since by man came death, by man came also the resurrection from the dead. For as in Adam all die, even so in Christ shall all be made alive." Vid. 1 Cor. xv.

The belief of a future state of existence, is absolutely necessary to strengthen the power of self-denial; to incite to the practice of disinterested virtue, and to refine benevolence from the pollutions of selfishness. * I agree

---

* Christianity does not propose entirely to extinguish the principle of self-interest, but to alter it's direction, and by urging us to forego a less or temporal self-interest, which repofes with the dust of man in the grave, to aspire after an interest ample as eternity. For this purpose, it constantly places before our eyes the crown of glory that fadeth not away;—it points to a state of happiness beyond the grave, exempt from corruption and

with Mr. Godwin, that men may be brought to act from disinterested motives, and that their general conduct may be regulated on a system of pure benevolence, but I deny that the principle which he assumes can ever produce this effect; nor can any principle whatever, whose operations are limited within the horizon of this life, and have no relation to a state beyond it.

The only possible way, in which to make men act from motives of pure benevolence, (as far as it respects personal considerations or worldly interest,) is by teaching them, universally to connect the idea of benevolence, and of every tender exertion of human kindness, with the hope, not of a present, but of a future and eternal recompense, with an interest greater than any which this world contains. To effect this, the belief of a future existence becomes an *essential requisite;* and this belief

---

decay; and teaches us to consider the temple of charity as the only way by which it is to be approached.

"Lay not," said Jesus with his characteristic simplicity of manner, "up for yourselves treasures upon earth, where moth and rust doth corrupt, and where thieves break through and steal. But lay up for yourselves treasures in heaven; where neither moth nor rust doth corrupt, and where thieves do not break through nor steal." Vid. Matt vi.

ought to be so impressed, as that the strength of it's conviction should, in a great measure, absorb every low, vain and sensual consideration.

Mankind cannot possibly be induced, by any the most specious argument, or theory, *which is relative to this life only*, to omit, in their dealings and intercourse with their fellow-creatures, the fond and captivating calculatings of present interest, and to practise a pure benevolence;—a benevolence, not prompted by temporal motives,—while they think this world the limits of their existence, the everlasting boundary of all their perceptions, their affections, their hopes and fears. But it is far different, when they look on this earth as the mere infancy of their being, and as a passage to another; where their happiness shall be proportioned to the degree in which they have cherished and have exercised the benevolent affections.

It may be said, that pleasurable sensation being the constant motive to, or object of human action, pure disinterestedness is unattainable by man. But let it be considered, that the belief of a future state does not tend so much to destroy the principle of self-interest, as to refine it from all it's base and polluted elements, and to sublime it into a pure and unalloyed disinterestedness, as far as any human and worldly recompense is concerned.

It must likewise be considered, that in the breast of the Christian, pleasurable sensation, ceasing to be a motive to selfishness, will be changed into the strongest motive to pure benevolence; for, the farther advances which the Christian makes in true holiness, the more he will esteem the joys of immortality, though at a distance, a source of purer happiness than any interest or possession on this side the grave.

Who has not felt, and been cheered by the kind solace of hope? Hope is an oblivion of misery, and a fore-taste of happiness. She gilds life in it's darkest moments; and makes the heart sensible to the touch of joy, even in the severest agonies. Were it not for this kind and seldom-failing visitor to the breasts of the wretched, mankind would sink into languor under the least affliction. It is hope, which gives energy to fortitude. It is hope, which keeps so many thousands of human sufferers light and buoyant above the waves of adversity. It is hope, whose benign and heavenly smile, administers cordial comfort to the prisoner in his cell, and the captive in his chains.—But to whom is hope so kind and constant a comforter as to the Christian? To whom does she impart such sweet or such lasting consolations? In other breasts, hope alternately lives and dies; but, in the breast of the Christian, she shines with immortal beams; and, instead of forsaking him in his last moments, she hails his closing eyes to the sight of "the everlasting hills;" and offers to his grasp "the crown that fadeth not away."

A PICTURE OF
CHRISTIAN PHILOSOPHY.

A few thoughts on the free discussion of the truths of revelation.

NO man's conviction, as far as it is rational, can be greater that the degree of his knowledge. Those who think otherwise, are only blind to their ignorance; and their presumption is folly. They are apt to be hardened in error, and to oppose a mere *ipse dixit* to the plainest arguments.

A man's faith in revelation, and of course his obedience to it's precepts, is usually according to his conviction of it's truth. But the truth of revelation, not being perceptible to the organs of sense, or capable of a palpable demonſtration, can only be aſcertained by diligent inveſtigation. Such inveſtigation of revealed religion was certainly intended by it's all-wiſe author; becauſe it's evidences are ſo arranged and modified, that there can be no conviction of it's truth without ſerious enquiry.

Had the Almighty intended to have precluded all diſcuſſion of the truths of revelation, he would have rendered it's evidence ſo clear, ſimple and indiſputable, that no two people could have differed on the ſubject. At preſent, there are no two people who think preciſely alike on all the points of Chriſtianity.

Why has the divine author of revealed religion permitted ſo vaſt a multiplicity of opinions on it's truth and doctrines? Certainly for the ſake of exciting enquiry, and of promoting diſcuſſion; for which there would have been neither neceſſity nor motive, if all men had thought alike on the ſubject. A complete uniformity of opinions might likewiſe, by promoting religious indifference, have been injurious to practical piety. The various ſhades of faith and degrees of conviction which prevail in the world, were likewise probably intended to teach us charity in our opinions, and humility in our judgments. Contented with our own conviction, we are not to imprecate anathemas on those who are not convinced in the same way.

If there be any to whom the evidences of Christianity may seem insufficient or inconclusive, from their wanting the inclination or the candour to give them a due and sober consideration; are we justified in persecuting them, either for their ignorance or their illiberality? Certainly not.——The genuine meekness of Christianity ought rather to incline us to behold their blindness with compassion, and their errors with forbearance: and to pray that God may open their eyes to see the truth; or may touch their hearts with that conviction of it's importance, as may make them examine it's evidences with seriousness and candour; and which cannot fail, in the end, of impressing their minds with faith in Christ Jesus.

Christians seldom pray with that fervor and sincerity which they ought, for the conversion of unbelievers.

They too often condemn them most uncharitably to damnation, without ever breathing a wish to heaven for their conversion to the light of immortality. The blessed Jesus evidently intended, that the conversion of unbelievers should make one of the daily petitions of believing Christians. "Thy kingdom come," is a supplication that Infidelity may vanish, and that the belief and the practical influence of Christianity may prevail in all the world. But with what sincerity can we utter this petition, while a bitter jealousy is rankling in our hearts; while we ourselves discover none of that mild spirit that was in Jesus, and rather strive to exasperate than convince the gainsayer?

If Infidelity have any arguments to produce against the truth of revelation, let them be calmly and rationally refuted: but if it can produce nothing but frothy abuse and virulent misrepresentation, the best reply is—that dignified silence and compassion which Jesus himself displayed, when he was rebuked and reviled. Can we follow a better example than that of Jesus?

Falshood and rancour always counteract themselves.

We are all convinced, that neither the sallies of wit, nor the perverseness of malice, can shake the philosophy of Newton. Should we punish the jackdaw for mocking the eagle? Have we any reason to dread, least the blasphemies of an individual should overturn the religion of the God of nature? The mere supposition is a disgrace to our belief. The scoffs of impiety cannot shake the fabric of heaven.*

---

* The writings of the infidel will not unfrequently be found to do more service than injury to the Christian cause. The frequent assault of the citadel, keeps the garrison awake. The attacks of the infidel, call forth the energies of the faithful, they excite arguments to strengthen the weak, or to confirm the wavering, which might otherwise never have appeared.

It is a very common, but a very mistaken supposition, that the writings of the French Deists produced that astonishing degree of infidelity that prevailed in France. Those writings were only a subordinate and secondary cause. The primary and essential cause, was the gross and palpable corruptions of the Romish Church. Those corruptions, accumulating for centuries, at last produced a monster that devoured it's mother. The Deistical philosophers might have hastened his birth, but they had no share in his formation. If the Deistical writers had been the essential cause of the declension of Christianity in France, the same cause, still operating, would have prevented it's revival. Christianity would have sunk, to rise no more! But there is the strongest proof, that the corruptions of the church and the clergy, rather than the scoffs of the philosophers were the cause of the prevailing infidelity in France: for the best informed travellers into that country assure us, that the infidelity

(261)

The Almighty who dispensed his religion to mankind, has, no doubt, provided, in the common order of things, for it's preservation; and it is full as absurd to suppose, that the Infidel can arrest the progress of revealed truth, as that he can stop the flowing of the ocean. The moral world, as well as the natural, has it's peculiar laws; though those of the latter are more open to our observation, because more familiar to our senses.

Man being constituted a free and rational being, the evidence of revelation was so disposed, as that it might controul his conduct through the medium of his judgment. It was a rule to him, not by constraint but by

---

itself is declining, now the cause that produced it is no more! The loathsome sensuality, the prostitute venality, and the splendid hypocrisy of the French church and the French clergy have vanished, and the religion of Jesus is beginning to appear with more of it's primitive simplicity. It it is now probable that Christianity will, in the course of a few years, when the present atrocious tyranny of the directorial ruffians shall have passed away, strike a much deeper root than before into the minds and the affections of the French; that the faith of the people, no longer cheated by the mummery of Popery, but founded on knowledge, will be immoveable; and that all the combined powers of Deism will be too feeble to do it any further injury. In this persuasion, as a Christian and a minister of Jesus, I feel a happiness that I cannot express; and I humbly implore the Supreme Disposer that it may not be illusory.

choice. Hence it's truth was proposed as an object of rational enquiry; and to this enquiry we are prompted by it's connection, not with a perishable, but an eternal interest; and which, consequently, renders it an object of superior importance to every human consideration.

Those who think that the truth of revelation ought not to be discussed, are by no means it's best friends. It's discussion seems to be an injunction of the Almighty, and designedly rendered necessary, by the very nature of it's proofs; and of this I am firmly convinced, that the more it is discussed, the more will it's beauty be unfolded and it's truth be displayed—the more will the love of it's laws and the conviction of it's importance approach to universality. Men ought not to be Christians merely from heresay or from fashion, but from conviction.— Every Christian should be able to give a reason of the " hope that is in him;" and those who cannot do this, though they may not be Infidels, hardly deserve the appellation of believers.

POSTSCRIPT

WITH that frank ingenuousness which is so congenial to a love of truth, and with that energy which a good cause always inspires, I have attempted to vindicate the combined, and (as I humbly think) indivisible interests of revealed religion, of free enquiry and of human happiness.* Instead of administering fresh fuel to that factious rage, and that spirit of bitterness which is

---

* The author has been scrupulously attentive not to contaminate this volume with any infusion of political animosity.—If the reader be anxious to be acquainted with his political opinions, he will find them sketched with plainness, with sincerity, and with moderation, in "An Address to the People, &c." 8vo. 1s. 6d. Rivingtons, and White. This little work which has been commended by critics, of a well-earned celebrity, (vid. Mont. Rev. Feb. 1799.) was written soon after Lord Nelson's victory, but (perhaps unfortunately for the author) the publication was delayed till Christmas; when the French arms, more destructive than the lava of Vesuvius, were preparing to revenge the losses of Aboukir in the plunder of Naples.

unhappily spreading through these once-happy kingdoms, I have endeavoured to soften the animosities of faction by the precepts of benevolence, and to inspire even the breasts of bigots with Christian moderation.—If I have contributed only a mite to this great end, it will cheer with many gleams of pleasure the bosom of one, who, in his way through life, has had much mournful experience of it's vicissitudes; and who can truly aver, that he never heard, without a wish to sooth, the piercing cries of human misery.

www.ingramcontent.com/pod-product-compliance
Lightning Source LLC
Chambersburg PA
CBHW021958220426
43663CB00007B/866